D1630413

MIXED UP

MIXED UP

TINEKA SMITH AND ALEX COURT

Copyright © 2021 Tineka Smith and Alex Court

The right of Tineka Smith and Alex Court to be identified as the Authors of the Work have been asserted by them in accordance with the Copyright, Designs and Patents Act 1988.

Originally published as an Audiobook by AUDIBLE

First published in 2021 by
HEADLINE PUBLISHING GROUP

1

Apart from any use permitted under UK copyright law, this publication may only be reproduced, stored, or transmitted, in any form, or by any means, with prior permission in writing of the publishers or, in the case of reprographic production, in accordance with the terms of licences issued by the Copyright Licensing Agency.

Every effort has been made to fulfil requirements with regard to reproducing copyright material. The author and publisher will be glad to rectify any omissions at the earliest opportunity.

Cataloguing in Publication Data is available from the British Library

Paperback ISBN 978 1 4722 8698 7

Designed and typeset by EM&EN
Printed and bound in Great Britain by Clays Ltd, Elcograf S.p.A.

Headline's policy is to use papers that are natural, renewable and recyclable products and made from wood grown in well-managed forests and other controlled sources. The logging and manufacturing processes are expected to conform to the environmental regulations of the country of origin.

HEADLINE PUBLISHING GROUP
An Hachette UK Company
Carmelite House
50 Victoria Embankment
London EC4Y 0DZ

www.headline.co.uk
www.hachette.co.uk

To our dads, Mike and Robert,

who taught us race shouldn't determine

whom we love.

CONTENTS

INTRODUCTION

TINEKA

I'm Tineka Smith and this is *Mixed Up*. I'm a Black American woman and my husband is a White British man. We felt it was important to write this book about our daily struggles of being in an interracial relationship in order to shine an often hidden light on the racism and prejudice interracial couples experience every day – and not just from White people.

I believe many of these hurtful racial interactions towards us stem from racism but some also from a place of hurt, confusion and downright ignorance. In my thirty-three years I've lived in the USA, the UK, France and Switzerland. At the age of twenty-two, I left the United States and I moved to London to study journalism. It was in the UK that I would eventually meet my husband, a White British man. But it was also where I started to feel uncomfortable in my own skin. In the USA racial tensions have existed for centuries and when someone is being racist you often know it and they know it too. But in Europe I was astounded at the borderline or overt racist things people in my inner circle would say to me and truly think that what they were saying was OK. In Europe there seems to be a sentiment that racism is only a problem in the United States of America and in some ways I think that makes it more dangerous.

Some of the experiences we've had, people might not believe still happen today. I think some people might assume that if a Black and a White person are in a relationship, they have no problems when it comes to race. I mean, all you need is love, right? But it simply isn't true.

The critically acclaimed 2017 movie *Get Out* catapulted interracial couples into the limelight, and the film was a hit among people of all races. Joe Morgenstern, of *The Wall Street Journal,* hailed the film directed by Jordan Peele as 'powerful' because of 'its prime location at the intersection of horror and race'. The film presented issues about stereotypes and prejudices in a dance between overt and nuanced references: suddenly multiracial couples were trendy. They were cool. We said to ourselves, 'Yes. Finally! We are accepted.' Then, one month later, a Black man spat on me in the street after he saw me kiss my White husband. And that was a reality check.

When Barack Obama was elected president, there

was jubilation in the streets. Black people celebrated as one of their own had finally made it to the top. Despite a history of racism, oppression and hate, a Black man had become president of the United States. Yet, referring to Obama as a Black man was met with a chord of discontent from many White Americans.

I remember sitting in my university lecture hall when I received the news on my phone. 'Obama's president!' one person shouted. Claps, shouts, frowns and comments ensued. Yet, out of the noise, one voice rose above the rest. 'I don't know why you guys are so happy,' said a White guy in my class. 'He's not even Black. He's mixed race.'

A 2011 census in the UK showed that over one million people identified as mixed race. In addition to this, one in ten people were either married or living together with someone from a different race. And, according to the Pew Research Center, 10 per cent of the population, or 11 million people, have a spouse of a different ethnicity in the USA.

A study by the BBC estimated that by 2020 those figures could double, showing that while many view it as a contemporary phenomenon, interracial relationships are far from 'new' in the UK.

Mixed-race communities are one of the fastest-growing groups in the UK, according to Lucinda Platt, a professor of Social Policy at the London School of Economics and Political Science.

Now, a note on language in this book: we use the word 'race' to reference persons of different ethnic and racial backgrounds. Call it what you like, but when it comes to race, ethnicity or skin colour, acceptance is still an issue.

When it comes to accepting interracial relationships, the world has shown that it does not matter who you are either. Take the Duke and Duchess of Sussex, better known as Prince Harry and Meghan Markle.

Markle became the first woman of colour to marry a British royal. In 2018 one would think this momentous milestone would be met with open arms. Instead, the royal couple were ridiculed, trolled and denounced by not only the public but also the British media. Media outlets such as the *Mail on Sunday* published horrific comments about the couple with phrases such as 'the Windsors will thicken their watery, thin blue blood and Spencer pale skin and ginger hair with some rich and exotic DNA'.[1] Scathing commentary from outlets such as the *Spectator* cut deep, with phrases like:

'Seventy years ago, Meghan Markle would have been the kind of woman the prince would have had for a mistress, not a wife.' But this is 2020 – not 1950. And we should ask ourselves exactly what the *Spectator* meant by 'kind of woman'.[2]

The backlash towards Meghan being with Harry was so great that many people believe it influenced the couple in leaving their royal duties in 2020. And some attribute it to the overpowering prejudice from the British media and public – with some titles such as the *Sun* focusing a bit too much of its time and energy trying to prove to its readers that racism did not play a part in any way of what the media has dubbed 'Megxit'.

The world has changed, and while progress has been achieved, we must not let those holding on to the scraps of a racially segregated and erroneous past prevent us from moving towards a rich and diverse future. And that future includes interracial relationships and families.

When I first started dating Alex, and in the first few years of our marriage, race wasn't really so much of a topic or a problem. Yes, we had some friends that made comments about us dating outside our race but it wasn't until I started to realise who I was as a Black woman and started standing up for myself against inappropriate comments that we started to have problems – most of which was when Alex would not stand up for me when our friends made comments that I found to be racist, no matter how subtle, or couldn't understand how I felt when I had a racist encounter. And sometimes he would even defend the people who I felt offended by.

As the Black Lives Matter movement swept across the USA and into Europe following the horrific deaths of Black men and women at the hands of police officers, such as George Floyd and Breonna Taylor – two among many – I needed to raise my voice with others in the Black European community to highlight the underlying racism that is so embedded in European societies today. This brought up conversations between Alex and me that were uncomfortable and caused fights – but they were necessary. We have definitely become closer through our chats and sometimes fight about racism but, over time, I feel that Alex has learnt to address his White privilege and have a better understanding of the daily oppression that Black people like myself face. Sometimes Alex sighs or rolls his eyes when I start going into a monologue and sometimes a rant about race. But I always remind him that if it is this tiring to hear about it, just imagine how tiring it is to experience it every single day. Being in an interracial relationship during the largest civil rights movement in history is almost advocacy in and of itself. The Black Lives Matter movement has reminded many White people of the responsibility they have to educate themselves about inequality and race – and that it's not up to Black people to do it for them. But I don't feel like I can tell my White husband to go read a book or educate himself. As his wife, I feel like I have the responsibility to call out and explain behaviours that happen which my husband might not always see. And in a way now I feel like I'm the racial equality advocate in my own relationship. When Alex and I were married, I was not prepared for the disconnect between us when it came to race. I hadn't expected that it would be hard for him to understand me. I didn't think I would need to explain everything to him when it came to race and microaggressions, which can be described as intentional or unintentional cues towards mostly marginalised groups that communicate hidden prejudices or negative slights. Alex is someone who has travelled and is educated. But the road to him understanding race, his privilege and being sensitive to the aspects of being with a person of colour has not been easy. These were facets I didn't expect when marrying someone outside my race, and perhaps I should have. We are now witnessing a worldwide shift in the awareness of what it really means to be Black or a person of colour in the twenty-first century. But more than ever with interracial couples and families. Couples with different skin colours are being forced to question and reexamine the dynamics of their relationship and their perception of each other within our society. This is difficult – really difficult. It's happened to my husband and me. We view this global moment differently and feel the role we must play at this time is also different. We hope this book gives you an honest glimpse into how we've dealt with the tension of race in our relationship and our lives as well as the courage and insight to be anti-racist and advocate for equality and change.

ALEX

When Tineka and I started dating, then got engaged and married in 2015, we learnt a lot, just like many other couples do. It felt special to be with Tineka and learn about who she is, how she sees the world differently to me and also how her ambitions are different to mine. We gradually learnt through trial, error and argument how to give each other the space we need to be individuals and chase our own dreams while living as an interracial couple.

Yes, Tineka was the first Black person I dated, but her skin colour was just one of her many features and was not why I wanted to be with her. And when I got down on one knee and told Tineka I wanted us to spend our lives together, I was not excited to be marrying a Black woman, I was excited to be asking that question to a woman who understands me, cares for me and makes me laugh.

Proposing to Tineka made so much sense, but understanding the rest has not always been so simple.

We have experienced some challenging conversations with friends and certain family members who did not naturally accept us – a Black woman and a White man – as a couple. And we were surprised. So we started talking to each other about the way people responded to us. 'Did you see the look on their faces when you introduced me as your wife?' Tineka would sometimes ask me as we made our way home after an evening with friends or colleagues. She wanted me to know she had noticed, and she had felt the subtle discrimination, those comments that reveal judgemental attitudes. And she expected me to learn, adapt and stand up for her and defend our marriage. It was a challenging learning curve for me, especially as it felt surreal to be having these conversations in the twenty-first century – our present-day reality.

As you read these confessions, we hope you will keep an open mind. *Mixed Up* is an unusual creation – neither an autobiography nor a biography. We ask you to be patient and reserve judgement until both perspectives have been presented because this is not two sides of the same story. We have examined and tussled with the chaos of our experience and tried to untangle and reveal our interracial relationship in order to bring you learnings that hit home. Truths that you know sit inside your own mind but perhaps have not been drawn out and expressed.

We hope that different people will take away different lessons. Maybe you will see conversations that you have been a part of – confusing or painful exchanges as Black Lives Matter protests hit the streets near your home and changed your thinking on equality and your place in the world. Maybe you are in an interracial relationship yourself and you are going through a situation where you see things one way and your partner sees it completely differently. Maybe you are someone with a multiracial friendship group, or someone who has found themselves not being understood during moments when multiple ethnic groups are together. Or maybe this book contains conversations that you have witnessed because your son or daughter, niece or nephew is in a relationship with someone who is from a different race. See if you can relate to the struggles we have been through and learnt from. Whomever you are, our invitation in this book is to see if you can challenge your preconceptions, stretch your thinking and make a real effort to understand people who are unlike you because they have a different racial profile.

We ask you to lend us your brains and their critical faculties. So, let's get confessing . . .

1

AWAKENING TO RACISM

TINEKA

Confession: I don't believe people when they say 'I don't see colour'.

I had my first conversation about interracial relationships with my mother when I was ten. She is a short and quiet Black woman who is religious to a fault. And in my childhood I remember her talking to me about race just once. One day she told me about her only dalliance with someone outside her race, and her story has stuck with me to this day.

My mother was born in 1955 in New Jersey but her parents originated from a small town called Perry in Georgia, the peach state of the United States. Interracial marriage had only become legal in 1965 when she was ten, and even then its legality had not been adopted by all the states. In fact, Alabama – where my father is from – notoriously failed to officially change its stance on this until the year 2000. Given this legal mentality, it's not surprising that, within my family, there aren't other interracial relationships and so they haven't had to confront mixed-race relationships in a real way before.

When I was in the fifth grade, I had a major crush on a boy in my class. He had flowing dark brown hair that rested below his chin and was one of the few boys with a sense of humour I actually understood at that age. One day we had a thirty-second conversation for the first time, and I felt assured that this meant he finally liked me. I burst through the door of our home after school that day and exclaimed to my mom, 'I like someone in my class and he likes me back. He's White!' It's interesting to me now that even at the age of ten I felt the need to tell her he was White. Clearly even at that young age I had learnt that skin colour meant something to everyone; I just didn't understand why at the time.

My mom was in the kitchen making me a snack and I sat back on the couch of our living room and opened up my homework binder. Usually my mom wasn't home when I arrived after school; she drove two hours to work and back every day, so by the time she arrived home each evening, we had already eaten dinner with my dad. I was a 'latchkey kid', and having someone to talk to in the house between the hours of 3.30 and 5.30 p.m. was a treat.

My mom paused for a moment, then this almost sheepish look came across her face. She walked up towards me and said in her usual quiet voice, 'You know, I liked a White boy when I was young too. When I was in high school.' I didn't think she was saying anything unusual and I wondered why she seemed almost embarrassed talking to me about it. But what I didn't understand was that she was talking about the USA in the 1960s, when being with someone from another race was still a new concept, and one that was often met with shame from others. She went on to explain that this boy liked her as well. She said they *really* liked each other. But they both knew nothing could ever happen. They did not even need to utter a word. They *knew*. It just simply was not possible for them.

They both knew the persecution they would face if it became something serious. I remember how it felt to hear this. It made me feel unsure about the boy I liked. And when I went to school the next day and every day after that, I limited my interaction with him until we naturally no longer spoke to each other. While it probably wasn't her intention, my mom's story scared me. I think she just wanted to connect on some level in terms of feeling drawn to people not only within her race but outside it, like I did. I didn't want to be targeted at school for liking someone who wasn't the same race as me. This persecution still exists today, and in my opinion – even though more subtle – it is stronger than ever.

I grew up on the east coast of the United States with my mom, dad and sister, until my parents divorced when I was eleven. My half siblings from my dad's previous marriage were never really present in our lives as much as I actually wanted them to be. As the oldest of two sisters in our small family of four, having older siblings was always a cool idea to me. My father was a naval officer, which meant we moved around a lot. Changing schools and making new friends quickly became routine to me, and I took a comfort in it. Even to this day I'll move apartments every other year – convincing my husband about the excitement of a new area to explore and neighbours to meet.

My relationships with my parents have always been very different from each other; I'm able to trace their influence on the decisions I've made and the outlook I have on life, especially when it comes to race. My relationship with my mother has always been much more subdued, in terms of teaching or sharing her beliefs on life and relationships, while my father and I have always had a close but tumultuous relationship.

We are the most alike out of all of his children in looks and personality, which might go some way to explain why we've clashed in the past.

I have a few vivid first memories of my dad. One is when I was around three. We were home alone in the kitchen and I had asked him for some ice cream. My dad started taking it out of the freezer – reaching for the ice-cream scoop in a nearby drawer. As I reached out my hands to take the bowl my dad said, 'Now say "please".'

'Peapie,' I quickly responded.

'No no, say "PUH-LEEZ".'

'Peapie,' I said louder.

'If you don't say "please", you're going straight to your room.'

'Peapie!' I yelled.

'Go to your room now!' my dad shouted, and I quickly stomped upstairs, sobbing and screaming at the top of my lungs. Back in those days, I really did love ice cream.

I was confused as to why my dad was being mean. I was saying what he wanted but the words weren't coming out right. So I tried my very best and shouted from upstairs as long and as loud as I could in a sing-song type of cry – 'Peaaaaaaaaaapieeeeeeee

Peaaaaaaaaaaapieee!' And I shouted that for the next fifteen minutes. From that day on my dad has called me Peapie.

Another first memory – with a less endearing outcome that was so turbulent it affected our family for quite some time. I was sitting at home with my mom and I was around the age of four or five. She was combing my hair, which was thick, unruly and long, cascading down my back to right above my waist. My dad had come home and was in a very rotten mood. The sound of my crying and sight of my tears set him off. He became so annoyed at my behaviour he marched into the kitchen and grabbed a pair of scissors. Then he came up to my mom and me, gathered my hair in a ponytail and cut it right to my scalp – in one clean snip.

There was a silence of shock and then my mom lost it. She jumped up, screaming, 'What is the matter with you?! I can't believe you would do this to your own child!' My mom ran into the bathroom crying and my dad followed. There was muffled shouting and soothing sounds as I imagine my dad wasn't prepared for such a reaction from my mom. The whole time I stood staring, watching the whole thing play out in front of me like a scene from a dramatic film. But at that age I had no attachment to hair and didn't really understand the concept of it yet. So when my dad emerged from the room, I ran up to him, jumped in his arms and said, 'It's OK, I forgive you, Daddy.' Later on, when my parents would recount the story, my dad said that was the moment he felt awful that, after doing something like that, I would just forget it so completely and willingly. And I think that was the moment I really won my dad's heart. And so that began our relationship, one of immense emotion, drama and love, but of complete trust. And it is that trust that explains why my views about race and acceptance have been so shaped by my father; I believed anything and everything he taught me.

Our relationship hasn't always been an easy one – in fact, there were years we hardly spoke at all because of one fight or another. There was an expectation my dad placed on me as a child, which was one of no nonsense and perfection. As a kid, I never really understood why I had to have straight As, why he would get annoyed if I didn't pronounce a word correctly, or cry over something petty. But I think now, as I've grown older, I've come to understand that he was preparing me for the obstacles he knew I would encounter because of my race and gender.

My father is an ex-military Black man who grew up in the harsh reality of the American Deep South. A place rife with the remnants of segregation and racism from its past and present. His experience of racism growing up shaped how he spoke to my sister and me about it. He talked about race constantly, always asking me to think about how I would have to navigate my environment differently because of the colour of my skin.

We'd be sitting in a restaurant and my younger sister and I would start arguing – shrieking at the top of our lungs as we tried to steal food off each other's plates – when the other wasn't paying attention. 'Be quiet!' my dad would manage to yell in a skilfully hushed voice. When we were in public places, he always had a menacing way of scolding us through gritted teeth, his pearly whites appearing as a smile to any stranger walking by. 'Do you want these White people to think we're crazy?!'

Honestly, as a kid, I didn't fully understand what he was saying, although one rule he enforced sticks in my head even now. In my dad's Southern family, using 'ma'am' or 'sir' was seen as a sign of ultimate respect. 'Now don't you ever say "ma'am" or "sir" to your White teachers, do you understand?' my dad would tell me. 'You can say it to your Black teachers but not the White ones. OK?'

In the Northern states, I really never heard people using these terms in everyday conversation – unless my parents were talking to policemen who had pulled them over for one thing or another. In my childish mind I knew that something was going on with White and Black people, and because of that I wasn't allowed to say 'ma'am' or 'sir' to them (only the Black teachers – or to police), as that would make my White teachers think they were better than me because of their skin colour.

And every chance he got he would hand me a magazine while I sat in the back seat of his Toyota as he drove around town. My dad loves cars, and so these magazines were always car-related, which I never found interesting. 'Read that whole article out loud for me,' he would often say. I would then recite two pages of tiny print, pronouncing words I did not understand, while huffing and puffing in annoyance for having to read something I found boring.

'I make you do this so you can pronounce words properly and clearly. In this world White people won't respect someone with your skin colour if you're uneducated and cannot speak and write well. Do you understand?'

'Yeah,' I replied.

'No! You don't say "yeah", you always say "yes".'

Those were my first encounters with differentiating skin colour.

Yet the same man who taught me to be proud of my skin colour, stand up to White people who I thought were treating me wrong and understand that anything I wanted in this world I would have to fight for, was the same person who taught me that dating outside my race was OK.

We were driving home one day in another car of his, an oversized blue Ford pickup truck. I would always ask my dad why he needed a truck when he already had a car. He'd respond, 'Baby, this is Alabama. You need a pickup truck.' I had just beaten him in a game of thumb war – the game we played to entertain ourselves when stuck in a sea of traffic. As he consented to defeat, I started to gaze out of the window. 'Hey, I wanted to tell you something,' he said. 'You know I was thinking that one day you may end up marrying a White or Asian guy, or you know someone outside your race. At the rate which Black men are being thrown in jail . . . shucks . . . almost over nothing these days . . . you might not have a lot of choice. And there is nothing wrong with being with someone outside your race.'

'Uh, OK, Daddy,' was all I managed to say. I was seventeen. And in the Deep South I can say 'daddy' until I'm old and grey, and it is still OK.

I didn't know it then. I didn't understand the significance of his statement at that point in time. But that was the defining moment, when I knew that interracial relationships were just as beautiful as same-race relationships. I think if he hadn't said this to me, I would have continued to feel self-conscious about dating outside my race, and it would have taken me longer to realise it simply doesn't matter. I believe the way generational minds are shaped truly does depend on family. My parents were the only family members to talk to me about interracial relationships, and it made all the difference, potentially saving me from being on the precipice of racial narrow-mindedness.

So perhaps you can understand why I hate it when people say 'I don't see colour'. References to skin colour are embedded in our everyday lives; a Black child, like I once was, is taught how to navigate through the world because they have a certain skin colour. The world I'm living in is set up for the success of White people, and that navigation is all about finding ways to succeed against the odds. I have heard the words 'I don't see colour' uttered by people of different races and socioeconomic backgrounds. I myself have spoken the phrase, while cringing inside at my own hypocrisy. I understand that people often use the expression to say that they don't judge others based on the colour of their skin. But by speaking those words we are ignoring the historical struggles, cultural differences and experiences that make us unique. I love my husband, but I am aware that he is White. I can *see* that he is White. And while his skin colour doesn't encompass my every thought, we do have conversations about race and how our day-to-day lives differ because of it.

White parents may often avoid the topic of race because they believe it's a taboo subject, and think that if they avoid it altogether, their children will grow up believing that skin colour is insignificant, that they 'don't see colour'. But, unfortunately, it has the opposite effect. A study called *Racial Relations Between Colorblind Socialization and Children's Racial Bias*, carried out by the Society for Research in Child Development, revealed that the majority of White parents tended not to mention racial issues when reading books to their children – despite it actually being the main aspect of the story.

In the US, where bigotry runs rampant, minority families have no choice but to talk to their children about race and prepare them for what they may encounter, and in the UK, while some may say the issue is more subtle, this still rings true. Yet it is also important for minority families to teach their children about accepting White people in a world where it can be very easy to become angry with the oppression and microaggressions minorities face on a daily basis. Because if we separate ourselves – which is very easy to do – the problem will only fester. A temporary Band-Aid for a growing infection.

Every day I fight this angry feeling bubbling inside me when I hear the news about the countless injustices minorities face. And, to be completely honest, I fight the urge to look over at my husband with a feeling of bitterness. This is not because I envy him but because he lives a life that is both consciously and subconsciously calmer and easier because society has shaped the world to benefit someone who looks like him. I am proud to be Black, but it can be overwhelming to live in a society where you are invalidated every day. We are bombarded by images of White people: in magazines, billboards, on TV, at work, even in greetings cards, and no matter where you look there is almost no representation of anyone who looks like you. It is a daily affirmation that society does not consider you 'normal'. So, teaching children about race is not supposed to be easy; it is just the right thing to do. In a world of diverse races and cultures, it's vital that White children learn the reality of race, and to appreciate differences and diversity at a young age, so that when they are older they are aware of their privilege, understand racial acceptance and are able to be racial allies. The next generation of White children has the ability to bring our society one step closer to racial equality and harmony, if only their parents will teach them.

Some time ago, my dad was close friends with a colleague of his, a White man. This man had a three-year-old daughter, and one day she came to visit him at work. When my dad approached her and extended his arm for a handshake, she exclaimed, 'Ewwwwwww! What's that stuff all over your hand?!' My dad glanced at his hand and asked, 'What stuff?' Then she cried, 'Ughhhh! It's all over your face too!' At this point my dad and the rest of the colleagues started to realise what she meant and broke out in a fit of laughter – including my dad.

On hearing this, I assume that the majority of White families do not talk to their children about race – and probably wouldn't know what to say. So, when my White friends ask me questions, I feel like I'm making up for the years they should have been taught about the very questions they ask. I have friends who had questions simply unanswered because they never had a Black friend to ask and their parents didn't help. These questions weren't offensive, and more often than not they would help them be more sensitive when it came to race and rhetoric. During an American History class in high school, while going over the Civil War, a White classmate leant over her desk and whispered to me, 'Hey, is it OK to call Black people "coloured"?'

I was silent for a moment as I wasn't quite sure if she was joking. Everyone in the class was seventeen or eighteen. I had expected her to know better, to have some sense of the reality of the world she lived in. I mean, we were sitting in American History class talking about slavery and the Civil War – the answer to her question was pretty apparent to me. But then I realised she was serious, and I thought, *Perhaps I should say yes, so that she learns her lesson when she says it to a random Black person.* But I saw the confusion in her eyes and the genuineness in her voice and I thought, *Wow, she really doesn't have a clue.* I let her know it would be a very bad idea to go around calling Black people 'coloured' and she happily said, 'Oh, OK!' and that was it – almost as nonchalantly as if she had asked me for the time. This was one of my first instances of having to educate a White person. I didn't feel any kind of way about it then, but as time went on and I had to do it again and again, it became apparent to me that there is a real problem of racial understanding or misunderstanding within our society that needs to be addressed – although I have learnt that, many times, some White people do not actually want an education.

Brigitte Vittrup, a psychologist specialising in child development at Texas Woman's University, shows in her 2016 study *Color Blind or Color Conscious?* that children start recognising skin colour as toddlers. Around this age, they are also developing their own ideas about racial dominance and will be influenced by racial stereotypes from teachers and other schoolmates. The study found that White children whose parents didn't talk to them about race were unsure if their parents would be OK with them socialising with someone from a different race or believed entirely that their parents would not accept them socialising with minorities.

'Color-blind ideology may actually do more harm than good,' says Vittrup. 'While parents may assume that their own egalitarian attitudes will rub off on their children, this is usually not the case. In one of my studies I found that children were more biased than their parents, and there was no direct association between the parents' and children's attitudes. Because when parents refuse to breach the subject it can transfer racial bias to younger generations.'[3]

Because when parents refuse to broach the subject it can potentially transfer racial bias to younger generations.

The study revealed that more than 50 per cent of White children surveyed in the US said they actually didn't know if their parents liked Black people, and 35 per cent asserted that their parents would not approve of them having a Black friend, or did not know if their parents would approve – despite their parents reporting positive attitudes towards those of a different race.

Remaining silent opens the door for prejudice. Our first ideas and concepts are formed as children, and that means conversations about diversity from our parents are crucial during this period. If families avoid discussing race, then children will pick up stereotypes from other sources, such as the media and friends.

If children have a positive understanding of colour, instead of when they see Black people portrayed as drug dealers, East Asians portrayed as kung fu masters and White people portrayed as the smart, successful scientists on television, they are less likely to be influenced by these stereotypical examples.

In society today it is easy to find preconceived notions of what it means to be Black or White. And this is perpetually reinforced by societal influences such as the media. Growing up, I was labelled 'White girl' by friends and certain family members because I spoke 'well', went to ballet classes, played the violin and did well in school. The constant commentary on how I wasn't 'Black enough' really tore at my identity and understanding of race. I was often made fun of because I talked 'too White', would speak up in class or because kids paid me to do their homework, which meant I was smart – and it was much cooler not to care about school.

'What do you want? An A, B or C?' I'd ask my customers.

'I was thinking an A,' one of them replied.

'You've gotten C's all year, it might look weird to the teacher,' I said.

'OK. A solid B then.'

'OK, that'll be two dollars,' I said, holding out my hand.

The reality, however, was that I didn't want to go to university. The reason was not because I didn't value it enough. I wanted to be a ballet dancer, and this was a dream I harboured well into my late teens, reaching a pre-professional level before graduating high school.

My mother was fully supportive of me practising ballet recreationally, but when I informed her at seventeen years old that I planned to audition for entry into a few ballet companies in New York, she immediately stopped paying my fees as a means of ensuring that I refocused on getting a degree. Education was non-negotiable. It was that simple.

I come from a middle-class family, but my parents grew up in working-class households, and at a time when Black people could most dominantly flourish in society by means of education. My parents wanted me to take advantage of the opportunities that they had worked hard to secure for my sister and me –

opportunities that weren't easily available to them when they were young. There are still large gaps when it comes to academic achievements between Black and White students. Astronomical tuition fees, poverty, White privilege and a lack of opportunities and access to thorough education have all contributed to the systemic disparity of successful and educated Black people compared to White people. I can understand why my parents felt that a university education was something that I had to achieve.

I strongly feel to this day that, had we been a White family, there would have been much less concern about how I could advance through life without several degrees. Eventually my master's degree led me to Europe, where I began to understand the similarities and differences of racism and microaggressions across the pond.

So yes, the statement 'I don't see colour' is a lie. Skin colour is all around us, and pretending to ignore it is futile. My husband and I know that we only have positive viewpoints of race because our parents taught us about skin colour. We were taught to be 'colour-conscious' not 'colour-blind'. And because I was taught to be colour-conscious, I knew the reason I had to go to university, talk a certain way and excel in school. Our parents taught us to be aware of the different colours and cultures of people around us, and to respect those differences with as much sensitivity as we knew how. It has made all the difference. There is nothing wrong with talking about race. So ask questions about what you don't know and explain the aspects you do. How else are we supposed to learn?

With all these experiences I've had, I know that I'm extremely lucky to have Alex's family as my in-laws, not just because they are genuinely warm and caring people, but because they have an understanding and sensitivity around race – more so than the majority of White people I have encountered. On one occasion, some family were sitting round the table for breakfast when I casually mentioned that I had read an article about the well-known actor Benedict Cumberbatch – aka Marvel's Doctor Strange – using the world 'coloured' to describe Black people and the backlash he had received. A distant in-law, who is White, asked, 'What's wrong with calling someone "coloured"? That's what you are, right?'

Their partner responded before I could. 'Remember that's not a word you're really supposed to say?'

But they continued. 'Being coloured is the same as being African-American.'

Several people shook their heads in disagreement. And then I spent around three minutes explaining history, slavery and oppression, and that the word 'coloured' was 'given' to us by White people in a time of overt inequality and injustice, and that, in general, Black Americans don't like to be called 'coloured'. I could have gone into how it's politically correct to refer to minorities as 'persons of colour' instead of 'coloured'. But this comment exposed a certain entitlement and an attitude that my culture was up for debate. The assumption that this person somehow knew more about being Black than me, was just too overwhelming and infuriating to engage. There are just some people you cannot get through to, and in that moment I decided to accept that insight rather than get angry. And so the conversation ended. There wasn't an acknowledgement that I was right – it just ended. And a feeling of relief seemed to wash over the room as everyone quickly moved on from the subject.

Racism and negative racial stereotypes surround us every day, but it still seems to be that the majority of White people – who benefit from racial privilege – are often too distracted by their lovely rose-tinted glasses to see the inequality and oppression that happens on a daily, if not hourly, basis. And I am learning that sometimes, even if I don't want to – even if I shouldn't have to, and it is in no way my responsibility – I end up having to teach those around me about what is right and wrong when it comes to race. And I always wonder if they really take what I say to heart or nod their heads for appearances only. This is not to say that all my conversations on race with White people are a negative experience. In fact, I would say I've learnt a lot in terms of perception, education and understanding. But, most of all, I have learnt there is a lot of sheer ignorance. We must talk about racism; avoiding it for the sake of White fragility will get us nowhere. With racial privilege comes a responsibility for White people to hold each other accountable. A racist joke? Don't chuckle – speak up. In the past I've witnessed on numerous occasions when a White person tells a racist joke and won't listen to my admonishment. They'll only back down when another White person comes to my defence. At the same time some of the people I've encountered who have shared their inappropriate opinions with me have very slowly changed their perceptions and understandings of why the things they say are wrong. This gives me hope and makes me see that, while it is a struggle, uncomfortable conversations about race really are worth having. We might not be able to make all White people understand, but I truly feel that changing the viewpoint of even one brings us a step closer to equality and unity.

2

RECOGNISING MY WHITE PRIVILEGE

ALEX

I am a White man. This is the demographic that occupies the majority of positions of power in all kinds of institutions and the demographic that has benefited from an elevated status in most Western and many non-Western societies throughout history. As you may know, the patriarchy is still a real thing, and White privilege is still a real thing. The combination of these truths means that I have lived many experiences from a privileged perspective. Our society can only really come together and benefit from all the diverse talents and ideas that exist if White men from different walks of life play an active role in breaking down the illusion of status. The first step in making that a reality is simply what I am doing now – recognising my own status and my own privilege.

While growing up I saw White men in all sorts of positions of power. Super-celebrated film stars, heroic sports players, politicians and business owners. Growing up was not hard for me. Not really. Of course, at the time, going through puberty and dealing with it all felt difficult, but when I look back on the experiences that I had, and the opportunities that were served up, I see that I followed a path that had been made smooth for me. The people I looked up to in my daily life not only looked like me, they expected me to behave like they did. It was easy to imagine following in the footsteps of those people who looked like me, came from families like mine and had similar concerns and priorities as me. Consequently, when people expected me to achieve certain things, I would attain those achievements. It was expected that I would get good grades in school. It was expected that I would play sports and have a group of mates who would help me through the ups and downs of teenage life. It was expected that I would have a girlfriend and I would break her heart because that is what boys do. Most chapters of my childhood and boyhood sync with what happens to most White men: they get what they want. Until recently I didn't have the tools to question this reality, but I am challenging myself and I am beginning to see that I personally benefited from living in a world that felt like it was made for me.

Even though I was taught about racial discrimination during history classes at school, it took me *years* to combine the teachings from my friends and family, and then connect the dots and see that my everyday life was anything but normal. And it took a lot of soul-searching to see that even my expectations were skewed by my privilege. It was only when I entered the workforce in my early twenties that I was really forced to confront my privileged status as a White man. Through jarring experiences in the office, I got a chance to peek beyond the curtain of my perspective and see with my own eyes what discrimination looks like in the real world.

About ten years ago I was fresh out of university, full of excitement to join the world of work and earn a salary. Righteous and naive, I sent my sparse CV to any newsroom that had a junior opening. I applied to regional newspapers, as well as the BBC, CNN and national newspapers like the *Sun*, *The Times* and the *Independent*. Someone at a major financial news network saw my CV and invited me to their London offices to interview for a trainee position. I read as much financial news as I could, put on my most professional clothes and went into the City.

At that time this company's newsroom was in a beautiful historic building near all the big banks, and it was a daunting experience just entering the place. Busy people in smart suits rushed past huge TV screens displaying the latest news on stocks, shares and investments. I joined a short queue for the reception desk and waited my turn, rehearsing in my head what I was going to say to the White blonde lady who was running the reception. 'My name is Alex Court. I'm here to interview for the trainee position.'

There was a woman in front of me in the queue waiting her turn. She looked a similar age to me. I guessed she was African or Afro-Caribbean, and she seemed nervous. I watched her slowly approach the desk and say something. The only response she got from the receptionist was, 'What's that?' After some explaining, the receptionist understood what was happening, handed her a badge and pointed her towards some escalators, which led deeper into the labyrinth. When I approached the desk moments later, the receptionist had a wide smile and asked, 'How can I help you, sir?' I delivered my well-practised line, which included my name and intention, and she said, 'Of course, just let me print your badge.'

The short encounter stuck in my mind because this lady was so polite and kind. The way she treated me with respect helped me to relax.

With my security badge dangling round my neck, I made my way to the interview room to find a group of ten to fifteen people. The candidates were an international mix of men and women from various ethnic backgrounds. I spotted the lady who had been ahead of me in the queue and was surprised to learn we were in the building for the same purpose. So why had the receptionist been confused? It was a thought that flicked through my brain without any interrogation or proper reflection. It didn't occur to me that maybe the receptionist had treated us differently because of our skin colour or our gender profiles. This was a professional place, I thought, where the best idea wins no matter whether it comes from a man or a woman, White or Black, the boss or the intern. Yes, like I admitted earlier, I was naive.

The sessions sped past, with presentations, group challenges and then a one-on-one interview. As the day progressed, I got into my stride. My confidence grew as the tasks made sense, and I felt that I could fit in at this company, build a network, earn some money and make my parents proud.

The hiring team was very positive at the end of the day, and just a few weeks later I recved an email that informed me I had been offered the trial position. I was going to be working with that team for ten weeks and I was going to get paid. I jumped at the chance – another moment where I didn't apply any proper interrogation or critical reflection on what this meant. I saw nothing but opportunity ahead of me, no concern that it would be too difficult or that people wouldn't like me.

From day one I threw myself into the work. Perhaps ten or fifteen people had been interviewed, but they only kept four of us for the trial period. The four of us were me and three women: one White-British, one Spanish and one Indian-British. We all worked hard and got along, but an element of competition was always there alongside the friendly chats in the break room; we all wanted to get the chance to stay longer. There were early starts and late nights. I neglected my friends over the weekends and read the *Financial Times*, more interested in trying to understand why Greece was going through a sovereign debt crisis and what LIBOR was.

As the ten weeks came to an end, the big boss lady took me to one side and told me the news I was hoping to hear: I was a good fit for the team. The boss explained they liked me because I behaved the way people should in a busy newsroom, where getting the right information out quickly was the aim of the game. 'Just look at them,' my boss said, gesturing towards the women who were not going to be staying after the traineeship period. 'They don't even look like they know they're in a newsroom.'

I didn't try to defend the other team members or encourage the manager to see they had other skills. This was my moment, so I just smiled widely and nodded, and said how much I enjoyed learning from the team and how happy I was to be working there. It felt like my big break.

The candidates who had been rejected said they were pleased for me, and that they had decided it was not the right place for them to work anyway. From the way they delivered the message it seemed they were disappointed because they knew who I was, and they could see who they had lost out to. As I was considering their perspective on the situation, the memory of the woman from the queue came back to me. She had not even been offered the traineeship, while these other two women had not been awarded jobs at the end of the trial period. I had. Me, a White man.

There could be many reasons why they chose me, but it's hard not to draw conclusions. How did I react? It felt like I had made it through *Dragons' Den*, and, to be honest, my primary emotion was excitement. I didn't fly into a rage and demand this injustice be corrected. And I didn't barge my way into the boss's office and call her a racist misogynist. I didn't have a smoking gun. It was all so subtle, and nothing the boss had said had really been overtly racist or even rude. But it might have been at this moment that I began to notice a pattern that there was opportunity for someone with my profile here. Was it just a coincidence that in my short time at the company I had seen men get rewarded and women get rejected? These thoughts left me as quickly as they had arrived – I was just consumed by the happiness that I had a job. I was no longer an intern or a trainee. It felt like I had made it and I felt that glorious feeling of achievement – I had done it all by myself.

I don't think for a moment that the company had surreptitiously decided they wanted to hire a White man to do the job. I don't think there was some conspiracy. This was more subtle. It was not my skin colour in and of itself that got me the job. It was my attitude, my confidence when interacting with senior reporters, managers and skilled camera operators. I could be trusted to go out on a shoot and film an interview with big business leaders and politicians. With people like Boris Johnson, who was mayor of London at the time, and the former corporate boss

Sir Philip Green, chairman of Arcadia Group, a now collapsed retail company that sold brands you have probably worn – Topshop, Topman, Miss Selfridge and Dorothy Perkins. A man who has since been under fire in British parliament, fighting allegations of grabbing women's breasts and bottoms.

I may not have asked these powerful leaders questions that were as on point as a senior journalist, but the bosses knew I would arrive on time, look presentable and firmly shake hands with the right people. I practised speaking clearly and with an authoritative tone. I was living that familiar lie: fake it until you make it.

Why was I in a better position to do this work than the other people who had wanted the job as badly as I had? Not because of my White skin, but perhaps because of the privilege my White skin and gender afforded me. My whole life I had watched others like me succeed, and had, therefore, pictured myself succeeding. I acted confidently because I was comfortable in these corporate settings surrounded by other blokes who were also confident and self-assured. Years and years of feeling like I deserved a seat at the table is my White privilege, and that had grown in me and built my personality, which I believe was the defining factor in getting the job.

When you look at groups of large and powerful companies, you see some revealing trends. According to *Fortune* magazine, between 1999 and 2018 there were sixteen Black CEOs at the helm of Fortune 500 companies. In July 2020, *Business Insider* reported that only three Fortune 500 companies had Black CEOs. Below the top level, Black employees form approximately only 4.7 per cent of executive team members in the Fortune 100 and 6.7 per cent of the 16.2 million managerial-level jobs. Boil all this research down and what do we learn? That White men continue to dominate positions of corporate power. Armed with this knowledge, the next logical question is: *why?*

It is an uncomfortable reality that my status as a White man means I have actually benefited from prejudice. The distinguished academic Dr Peggy McIntosh explains this excellently in her seminal paper *White Privilege: Unpacking the Invisible Knapsack.* She said, 'As a White person, I realised I had been taught about racism as something that puts others at a disadvantage, but had been taught not to see one of its corollary aspects, White privilege, which puts me at an advantage.'[4]

I am still learning, by reflecting on how my experiences and achievements may not always have been down to my hard work, because I can now recognise this privilege and see how it has helped me along the way. Would I have become conscious of it had I married a White woman? Probably not.

Understanding this perspective is not easy, because it muddies my memories; my proudest moments are perhaps not what I had thought they were, because I got so much help. My parents encouraged me every step of the way, my brothers and my sister too. And, of course, all kinds of friends. But the support did not stop there. My professors at university, and my school teachers before them. It is a privilege to have that feeling of being supported; it really is a special thing. But I also know that everybody deserves to feel that way, and that isn't the case. The acclaimed actor Wendell Pierce, who starred in *The Wire*, has given an exceptionally personal insight into his experience growing up in New Orleans. In a recent radio interview with BBC Radio 4 he put it like this:

> 'Being in the Deep South, a little black boy growing up is told, if not directly, indirectly that they are sub-par, that they are not enough, that they are

less than, that you aren't valued . . . I felt alone at times, as though I was less than.'[5]

Pierce says he had to fight against the societal tide to realise he was someone of purpose and promise, and that is especially astounding as he has inspired so many people through his acting. His contribution has made changes in society, and because of his work others will not have to experience the feelings of self-doubt he went through. And hearing those words from him is very humbling for someone like me, who never had to fight that battle, overcome those feelings and that pain. It is an important message, even though it is a challenging one. This interview with Pierce reminded me how we need to listen to these stories and personal histories to form our own behaviour, break down barriers and remove discrimination wherever we encounter it.

I have faced this challenging learning curve head-on through my marriage with Tineka. And many difficult lessons have been learnt as I have watched my wife experience racial aggressions.

Not long ago, Tineka and I entered a well-known clothing store in downtown Geneva, Switzerland. It was a fancy outlet with leather jackets on display next to ripped jeans and vintage handbags. Tineka and I went to different parts of the store, and we had been casually browsing for only a few minutes before Tineka appeared next to me. 'We're leaving,' she hissed into my ear.

She stormed out of the store, giving the shop assistants a harsh stare, and then told me what had happened. The two White female shop assistants had taken a very close interest in Tineka and had followed her as she browsed the shelves. 'Isn't that their job?' I had naively asked, only to be asked whether a shop assistant had done the same to me, which of course they hadn't. 'I wish shop assistants would assume you are the thief for once,' Tineka replied, clearly upset.

My wife had been labelled and treated suspiciously, made to feel uncomfortable because of her skin colour. She had then decided she wasn't going to put up with it, and removed herself from the situation before she got angry.

As I watched her walk off, I was frozen at the store entrance, hoping that I would somehow find the courage to go and confront the shop assistants. I wanted them to understand what they had done and recognise the very real consequences. But I also knew that I didn't want to be that White man who spent his day mansplaining – telling women how to act in a racially sensitive way. The hypocrite who makes zero positive impact but comes off looking like a fool. As Tineka looked back and saw me hesitating, she gestured to me, telling me to let it go. I am not pleased to admit that I felt relieved. As I caught up with her, I went to give her a hug, but she wasn't ready for that kind of comfort, and we just walked together silently. As the scene played over in my mind, I realised I was also pissed off by how rude and insensitive these people had been. Partly, my anger came out of a lack of understanding – *why* do people behave so badly? Surely, it's easier to treat everyone equally.

Being in an interracial relationship has challenged me to confront these experiences and feelings head-on, and initially that terrified me. I wasn't ready to define who I was through how I acted in negative situations. Is the person I want to be the type of person who gets upset and angry in these moments of reality? Or is the person I want to be able to rise above this ignorance and move forward with living life? It is really challenging to answer these questions, because I want Tineka to see that I care, and I want her to feel like she has an ally in the person she married. But these situations I have experienced vary so much in intensity, and I am just like everyone else – I have my good days and my bad days. Sometimes I can find the patience I need to deal with ignorance, and other days I get pissed off and I can't hide how I feel. On other days I feel weighed down by our judgemental society. It's complicated, but these experiences have taught me a great deal, and I have developed in my approach to the world around me: now I have different expectations from people, fewer expectations.

I have also found more meaning in my own experiences by reading about how other people witness and interpret inequality and racism. Words from the author and columnist Charles M. Blow, published in *The New York Times*, resonated with me:

> 'I believe that too many of our white neighbors are choosing to be intentionally blind to the enormous breadth and scope of racism in this country [America], because to acknowledge it would be to condemn self, family, friends and community. It would be to recognize that much of their existence is privileged, and conversely blackness is oppressed.'[6]

I see this truth in my experience, because I ignored and denied my own privilege as a White man for many years. Blow's words also spoke to me because the reality is that we treat racism differently when it comes from different people. If someone I am close to – a friend or a family member, for instance – makes a comment that is ignorant or racist, I am most likely to not hear it, or not recognise it for what it is, or just simply excuse it. I am more likely to move the conversation along and brush over the words to prevent an argument. Whereas if I read that an elected official has treated a Black person with disrespect, or if a colleague makes an ignorant comment, then I am more likely to be outraged and upset. It is not fair, but I do see myself in this reality that Blow identified. His words made me realise that standing up to those people who are closest to me is really difficult – but vital. It would take enormous courage to confront a close friend and tell them they are acting in a racist way because the consequences hit so much closer to home.

Moments of discovery – like Tineka being treated with contempt in a shop – have taught me to think differently about how I confront racial discrimination. After careful thinking, I have identified three different phases.

At first I would witness a microaggression and I would not even realise what had happened. I was literally blinded by my ignorance and my inability to assess what was going on through a racial lens. Secondly, I experienced a period when I would see White people treat my wife in a judgemental way and I would explain away the problem in my own head. My thinking was along the lines of: *There must have been some kind of misunderstanding* . . . And finally, I have started to see just how much pain can be inflicted by ignorance. The way I treat other people and the way people treat me can have a momentous impact, and there is no escaping that.

Moving through this process has been one step forward, two steps back, but I have come to feel less pain or anger. What I do experience when I witness racial microaggressions, however, is a deep sense of disappointment. Even generally compassionate and intelligent people can perpetuate stereotypes, all while being incredibly unaware of their behaviour, not realising that it reveals so much about their own insecurities regarding other people, other cultures and other races.

My gut instinct is to do something about these emotions, but what exactly would be adequate? Tineka has told me time and time again that we have an opportunity to educate people we know about racism and the right way to treat people who are from minority groups, but I often have a feeling that those people are not worth my breath or my time. Putting it like that makes me sound lazy or scared, but I have seen people behave in ways that are so baffling and at odds with my values that I think the only way to respond is to walk away.

Making this judgement call is a conundrum that has resulted in numerous discussions, conversations and arguments, which often boil down to three deeper core questions:

Question 1: Do I hope to change racial stereotyping?

Question 2: What sort of husband am I?

Question 3: What kind of person am I?

And, let's be real, who has ever really been able to answer those big ones?

I do not find it natural to fly into a rage or insist others see things from my point of view. But I have confronted my fears and I am trying to develop a strong racial awareness as I have tried to grow into a husband who is prepared to fight the right fight alongside his wife. I have taken a hard look at myself and realised that I must do more and make concrete steps to grapple with an issue that is outside my comfort zone, outside my experience and outside my immediate reality. As I have said, it is a process and a journey.

Confession: When our cultures clash, I feel overwhelmed.

Christmastime in Birmingham, Alabama. Not Christmas Day itself but a few days after. We headed into my wife's grandparents' house to find a little gathering of family and close friends who were very excited to see Tineka and hear about her life in Europe. We were treated to big American hugs and plenty of food. I had never been to this house before, and many of the people there were relatives I was meeting for the first time. There was so much for me to take in, but the scene somehow felt familiar, like what I know about American households from TV.

We got to chatting and I was trying to concentrate and answer questions, but I could really only focus on one thing. Hanging on the main wall in the living room was a very large framed photo. It was the only decoration on the entire wall. It was not of family, or grandchildren graduating from high school. The only photograph this elderly couple had mounted on their living room wall was of Barack and Michelle Obama. It was an official photo, very staged, with proper lighting, and I thought it would fit in well on a wall in an embassy or some other government building.

I was gobsmacked, but how should I react? I wanted to talk about it and ask my in-laws about it, but I was also very aware that I was the only White person in the room. The last thing I wanted was to embarrass Tineka or for anyone to think I was ignorant. There were always loads of photos in my parents' home, but I grew up surrounded by photos of family members, not politicians. But now I felt conscious that I was in a house owned by people who had grown up during a time when a Black man had no chance of becoming president of the United States. The 2008 presidential election was a huge deal around the world, including in the UK, but this all happened before I met Tineka, and I remember watching the events unfold fairly casually with my mum and dad. In reality we didn't have much skin in the game. But for my wife's family it was so momentous that they wanted a photo in their living room, something that was a daily reminder that things had changed.

My guess is that the election itself was overwhelming for my wife's grandparents but being in their home and bearing witness to the way they expressed this feeling was overwhelming for me. Never would my family be so overt, especially about politics. But when I get to thinking why that is, I see the significance is perhaps not so political, but personal. Ever since I have understood what British politics is, there have been senior cabinet ministers and prime ministers who are White, middle-class, well-educated people like me. The Queen is a White person, the royal family has always been White and we are only beginning to see some change to that established power now that Prince Harry, the Duke of Sussex, has married Meghan Markle. While this has caused shockwaves, there have been moments before my time where the game changed in the UK. Britain elected the first female prime minister in 1979, and that was momentous in many ways. Prominent politicians in the UK who are not White include Paul Boateng, Diane Abbott and Chuka Umunna. They are among a group of influential people who have made a significant contribution to British life by reflecting the diversity of modern Britain in the Houses of Parliament. But the Obamas have challenged the very structure of US culture and living through this change was clearly a huge deal for Tineka's grandparents to experience. The election of Obama meant there was finally someone at the highest level of power who was closer to their reality. Someone who could do a real job of representing them and their people in a way that would make them proud. How a family reacts to this kind of radical change is complex, but this family was doing things totally differently to what I knew.

Getting to know your partner's family has its complexities all over the world. I know people who can't have a conversation with their in-laws because they don't have a language in common. But I am regularly surprised at just how different my family dynamics are compared to those of my wife's. I have seen how family time behind closed doors has a different meaning on different sides of the Atlantic Ocean, and that is partly due to race, partly due to culture and partly to do with family dynamics, personalities and upbringings.

My family has never included half-siblings or step-siblings. My wife has one sister and three half-sisters who were born during other marriages. My family has never lived with foster children. My mother-in-law gave shelter to two young kids who came from a truly broken home. Those are just two, but there are many factors that make us different clans. So, when the time came for my family to meet my in-laws for the first time, I didn't know how it was going to work out – my White British family and her Black American family. Both families have travelled and been exposed to international experiences, but I still wondered whether there would be instances of 'lost in translation', given the international and interracial aspects of the meeting. And Tineka and I spoke about these anxieties. I told her how badly I wanted the two families to get along, and how I wanted my parents to be the chilled-out people they are most of the time. I guess I was nervous because, throughout the years, my parents have placed a lot of emphasis on etiquette and taught me to act correctly, which can seem uptight to some people. For example, I told Tineka about the bell system my parents had used to call the children for family meals. In every house we lived in there was always a small brass ship's bell mounted on the wall near the kitchen. My mum would cook a meal and then my dad would loudly ring the bell and summon the children to the table. It gave him great joy to ring the bell, and he did it with a wide smile on his face, even though my mum would cover her ears and tell my dad to stop being so loud. My parents were never mean, and they were not disciplinarians, but they had their way of doing things, their rules and their expectations.

I hoped they would hide this side of their personalities just a little when they met Tineka's family.

In the lead-up to the get-together, when these thoughts were rumbling through my mind, I had a different flashback to life as a child. I remembered my dad making a one-off comment that I had the choice of marrying a White person, an Asian person, a Black person, a woman or a man – and whatever I chose was OK. It was a rare moment with just the two of us, and he was concentrating on delivering a message that was simple, generous and open. What he was saying was that the decision was mine to make, and my life was mine to live. It just so happened that Tineka and her dad had a similar one-on-one conversation about these kinds of choices, and that conversation also had a big impact on Tineka.

From this perspective choices opened up to me, and that included people. Being taught how to be an open person from a young age, and to appreciate the value of choice, gave me confidence and a deep appreciation of diversity. While the conversation my dad had with me was short, it had an impact on who I am as an adult. And those values were reinforced on that day when our families met. When I saw my dad smiling and shaking hands with Tineka's dad, and saw my mum give Tineka's mum a welcoming hug, I saw real warmth and openness.

Sadly, not all gatherings have left me feeling so warm. In fact, I have been at several events which have been painful. For instance, when Tineka and I went to an office Christmas party a few years ago, I was seated next to a young White woman. As she pointed out who her partner was I realised this woman was gay. She told me more about her life and I was shocked when she told me that some people in her life had stopped talking to her because they did not agree with homosexual relationships. Eventually, I explained I was at this event with my wife Tineka and I pointed her out. I explained how we had met, where we lived and a little about Tineka's professional life. Then this woman grabbed my arm and looked me straight in the eye and said, 'I know you have trouble being married to an African-American woman. But, oh she is *beautiful*.' I was stunned. What kind of 'trouble' was it that I was having? It was obvious to me that she was trying to be empathetic and draw parallels between our situations, but I didn't think it was right for her to bring up my wife's skin colour. When I found my words, I managed to keep my cool and react calmly.

I told her that Tineka was very close with my parents and my siblings and that we were very lucky to have such a warm family who supported us and never judged Tineka based on her skin colour. She had wanted to tell me about issues she had faced by being in a same-sex relationship but she hadn't acted with the same respect – she hadn't given me the space to judge whether or not I wanted to tell her about *my* experience of being in an interracial relationship.

This situation felt bizarre, especially because we were in a friendly space, and suddenly someone I had just met was projecting her personal problems on to me and insuinating I was experiencing something similar. I stayed in my seat, and tried to be polite, but became increasingly interested in talking to the person on the other side of me. I was reminded how I have changed as a result of being in an interracial relationship. I realised that I might not have previously noticed some throwaway comment like this before. Not noticed what it really was. And I also found it confusing as to why this woman assumed she understood what Black people go through or what it was like to be in a relationship with a Black person.

After the event, Tineka and I headed home and got chatting about the evening – what we had eaten and who we had met. I was holding back a bit because I didn't really want to tell Tineka about the comment this woman had made. I didn't want Tineka to feel like she had been talked about and judged as the only Black person at the event. But it was on my mind, and I was thinking about what it is that makes other people think it's OK to make my wife a topic of conversation. This woman had picked up on one characteristic she could see in my wife and used that one thing, her skin colour, to make a raft of assumptions and then verbalise them.

I was reminded of the time when Tineka and I lived in a big apartment building and I got chatting to someone else who lived there. They had asked which apartment I lived in and when I told them the floor, he remembered, 'Ah, yes I remember seeing you. Your flatmate is Black, right?' That comment had also seemed rude and judgemental to me. Rude, judgemental and just unnecessary. Why did people feel they could say that to me?

As I was mulling these thoughts over, it seemed Tineka realised something was up with me. But before I could formulate my thoughts into words and tell her, Tineka let out a loud laugh. It turned out she had texted her dad a photo of the festive evening. His reply, which had tickled Tineka, was: *Look at you, so pretty there. The only speck in the milk.* I couldn't help but laugh with my wife. In that moment the tension I had felt from that unsettling conversation faded into the background, and I was reminded of the excellent guidance from Richard Carlson: 'Don't sweat the small stuff.' I could have chosen to blow the whole thing up and tell Tineka – 'OMG, you will not believe what this woman said!' – or I could keep things low-key and tell Tineka I felt a bit uneasy and slowly process what I had witnessed. This choice was mine to make, and I went with the second option.

Confession: It shocks me to see how the racism of the past built the societies we live in today.

The most arresting, painful and shocking history lesson I have ever received was not in a classroom. I came to understand just how powerful the past can be when I was on holiday, travelling around Ghana.

I visited the West African country with a friend while I was on my summer holiday from university.

Neither of us wanted to go to the nightclubs and bars of the Greek islands, so we chose Ghana; we didn't know what to expect, but we went with our eyes open.

When we arrived in the capital city, Accra, we found a hectic bus station and asked around until someone showed us what bus would take us into the city centre. People hesitated before answering our questions – they seemed surprised that two White boys would want to take a normal rusty suburban bus rather than an air-conditioned taxi. The locals didn't rush to get on board, and it was only when the bus we were on filled up with passengers that someone told us these suburban transports only get on the road when the driver is satisfied he can't cram another paying person into the vehicle.

While we were rolling along the highway, passing trucks and taxis, I became very aware that my friend and I were the only people on that bus who weren't African. For the first time in my life I stood out as member of the minority, and that was a new experience for me. I felt visible in a way I didn't normally feel, and that made me feel a bit isolated. I didn't wish for other White people to get on the bus and help me stand out less. I didn't feel the need to blend in, but at the same time I didn't want to stand out.

What was even stranger than this feeling of isolation was the reality that I didn't actually feel uncomfortable. This was a relief, but I now clearly see that this feeling is privilege. Having spent so much of my life in the majority and surrounded by people and experiences I could relate to, this feeling on the bus was a new experience. But because I was on the road, it all felt exciting, like an adventure that I should embrace before I returned home in a few weeks. This bus ride was a one-off, it was not my new life. It was important to go through the realisation that I was not having a similar experience to the millions of immigrants who live in the places where I grew up, and that is because of the more subtle aspects of discrimination. What I was experiencing was not the same as the daily reminders, the nagging questions of whether you are accepted, whether you belong. Questions and feelings that I had not been forced to confront. Questions that, if left unanswered, build up over time.

After a few days in the big city, we were ready for a change of scenery, and we decided to travel to Elmina. In the 1480s this town was a Portuguese trading settlement and an important slave-trading post in the region. In Elmina we checked into a simple hotel, showered and signed up to a guided tour of the town's tourist draw: the castle.

We enjoyed walking along the ramparts and feeling the sea air but the experience changed dramatically when our guide took us down a flight of crumbling stairs. Down below, the only light came from two small man-made cracks in the walls, and the place was sad, eerie and airless. The tour guide ushered our small group into one of the cells where African slaves had been held before the treacherous journey across the sea to their new lives working the fields of the 'New World'. When every member of the group had entered the cell, the tour guide slowly and solemnly clanged the door shut. Then, in the half-light, he asked the group to take some time in silence and remember where we were standing: a place with a history full of inequality, pain and brutality.

It was the longest two minutes of my life. My mind was racing, so many thoughts pinging around my brain about the sadness of it all. As I tried to concentrate and focus my thinking, one of the tourists standing near me let out a small sob.

I realised I was trying to comprehend how inhumane people can be. Our capacity to discriminate against one another and exact such suffering on other people. It made me feel sick. And I wondered whether we as humans have really learnt from this history or not. If this was possible hundreds of years ago, what brutality had we yet to come up with? Were we safe?

The tour guide told us that the best estimates say 30,000 slaves were traded every year in Elmina before slave trading was abolished. Those 30,000 people were mothers, sisters, children, sons, fathers. People who were tortured, abused and dehumanised because of the colour of their skin. Forced to live in a crowded cell, surrounded by human waste and human fear. And then those who survived the months of waiting, people who'd had their fight beaten from them, were marched through the door of no return on to the ships that would take them away from their homeland and everything they had ever known. They were ripped from their world and their societies, forced to travel like cargo to work the fields of the Americas.

Those moments in the dark cell in Elmina had a profound effect on me. They were the closest I have ever come to understanding the huge and devastating impact of the slave trade, which changed the lives of so many generations even after it was officially abolished. Only decades have passed since White people and Black people were officially segregated in the US.

In some parts of the United States the colour of your skin was the official signifier that determined which part of town you lived in, which section of the bus you sat in and which restaurants you were welcomed into. Your entire life and the kinds of opportunities you had were dictated by the colour of your skin. Societies and attitudes have since fluctuated, and laws have changed, but this history is neither dead nor buried. The past has affected generations, and continues to linger. The law might have changed, but the impact of this history is still being played out today.

My experience in Elmina came full circle for me many years later when I was standing in Tineka's grandparents' living room, looking at the photo of Barack and Michelle Obama. I have the luxury of not having the language or the shared heritage of my ancestors to fully understand what was behind Grandpop's decision to put the photo up. But even I could see that if the concept of a Black person being worth less than a White man had been so entrenched in society, it's no wonder that they felt driven to put up that photo when a Black man became president of the United States of America.

3

PREJUDICE DOES NOT DISCRIMINATE

TINEKA

Confession: Growing up, I was taunted by my Black friends and peers because of my dark skin.

While the Black community has made enormous strides in fighting for equality, some people have unconsciously bought into the stereotypes of what society determines is Black and what is White – leading to labels and taunting when people act outside our predetermined social constructs. This is more often than not encouraged by the media's portrayal of White people and persons of colour. In films you will rarely find a dark-skinned Black person playing the role of, say, a lead scientist – that will likely go to their White counterparts – or perhaps a lighter-skinned actor. The biopic about the acclaimed singer Nina Simone, aptly titled *Nina*, received backlash from the Black community when the light-skinned Afro-Latina actress, Zoe Saldana, was chosen for the role. She wore prosthetics to imitate Nina Simone's broad nose and full lips, while darkening her skin with make-up. This was a sad tribute to the famous singer who once said, 'I've never changed my hair. I've never changed my colour. I have always been proud of myself.' The fact that it was preferable for a light-skinned actress to play an iconic dark-skinned singer, who was not the standard of 'beauty' in her time, shows that Hollywood would prefer to give the illusion of blackness, rather than the reality. Reminiscent of a time when White actors would appear in films in blackface, as it was better to be a White person playing a dark-skinned Black person than to actually be dark-skinned.

This societal attitude towards dark skin certainly doesn't help how the ideals of beauty are interpreted within the Black community. Growing up, I was often made fun of by my Black peers about the shade of my skin – comments that I didn't receive as much from White kids until my older teenage years. Colourism, or shadeism, is a form of discrimination against someone based on the shade of their skin. This happens from people within the same race more than you would think but does not disclude those same attitudes from White people. I had the fortunate grace to have parents who constantly told my younger sister and me that we were beautiful and intelligent. And in all honesty, while I did wish I had lighter skin and straighter hair as a kid, the consistent affirmations from my parents – who knew nothing about the teasing I received, but could well have experienced something similar themselves – were a barrier against these comments ruining my sense of self, beauty and identity.

Ironically, the main kids making fun of me were often dark-skinned themselves, and they would make sure they'd do it loudly too. Others didn't really comment but would look on confused or smiling, thankful, I guess, for the entertainment between classes and the fact that they themselves weren't the ones being targeted. I think those kids did it because they were insecure about their own dark shade of skin – as being less White meant being less normal or beautiful – and wanted to distract others from it by any means possible. Even if it meant making fun of people who were the exact shade they were.

And in today's society it's no surprise. We're seeing this not only in America and the UK, but also more widely. The Oscar-winning actress Lupita Nyong'o, who was born in Mexico City and grew up in Kenya, has been vocal about her experience of colourism, stating that, 'We still ascribe to these notions of Eurocentric standards of beauty, that then affect how we see ourselves among ourselves.' Calling it 'the daughter of racism' in 'a world that rewards lighter skin over darker skin'.[7] Western culture is still very pervasive when it comes to skin colour other than White. Colourism is a virus that forms early in our childhood, created by the ideals of White supremacy and a society that places value on White skin – and deems it beautiful. This in turn teaches impressionable children who are not White or 'appropriately' light-skinned that they are not normal – in a sense they are 'outcast' with no sense of pride in their skin, identity or culture. Within our own communities we feed this, by praising lighter skin and 'good hair' – hair that is less nappy, longer and more European. As children and teenagers we pick up on this. We avoid going in the sun or we ask our moms for relaxers in order to have long, flowing hair that we can shake back and forth like the White women we see on television. Even high-profile Black figures are not shielded from the effects of colourism.

And it sits in plain sight within not only Black but other minority communities. On a typical day for me in a mostly diverse elementary school while I was living in New Jersey, a girl loudly announced in the hallway near our lockers, 'Hey, let's have a contest –

who has the darkest skin? I think it might be me . . . Oh, wait, oops, it's definitely Tineka.'

One guy – also dark-skinned – chimed in. 'Hey, Tineka, I bet your teeth glow in the dark.'

Most of the time I let it roll off my back. But sometimes they would get on my last nerve.

'WHAT ARE YOU TALKING ABOUT? YOU'RE JUST AS DARK AS ME!' I exclaimed one day.

They froze. One kid said, 'Uh-oh, Tineka's angry,' and the others just looked on. He had nothing to say because he knew it was true. But he had an audience, so he chuckled, swirled his finger in a circle by his temple to imply I was crazy and went to class.

I also experienced the effects of colourism from White friends and peers. In my predominantly White high school, where minorities were less than five per cent of the student population, colourism was more subtle. It was in high school that I started hearing comments from White peers. I was the only Black girl on the high-school basketball team. When the time came for the team photo, my dark skin was the centre of laughs and conversation. Even the coach laughed along as one teammate repeated the story the coach had told them about how the photographer had to add a green tint to the photo so I'd actually show up in the picture because I was 'so dark'. Other jokes such as, 'Look, Tineka's teeth are glowing!' when we were in dark areas became a norm. I know that they expected me to let the comments roll off my back and not make a fuss. And that's what I did – shamefully closing my mouth so they could no longer see my teeth.

But I think the most striking incident in my high school was the senior class photo. The White photographer was asking everyone to move in closer. She described students by their clothes or shoes or hair colour. But then she said, 'Hey, you, move in closer . . . the dark one.' I looked around because I was hoping she wasn't talking to me that way. Then she said it again, looking straight at me . . . so I moved in closer. Everyone else froze. The teachers said nothing. My friends said nothing. And, most importantly, the Black kids standing there said nothing. They just glanced at me, clearly embarrassed for me I guess, but not willing to say anything to the clearly inappropriate photographer. I wish I had the courage to speak up and say something then. I should have said, 'I have a name like everyone else here.' Or told her she could describe me by my clothing like everyone else. I wish I had said, 'It is absolutely inappropriate to describe me that way.' But I promised myself afterwards that I would take every opportunity I had to stand up for myself when I felt I was being mistreated, and be as loud and vocal about it as I could.

It's more important than ever that we teach all children and even more so ourselves that all shades of Black (and other ethnicities) are beautiful and equal. If, as a community, we want others to believe that and treat us as such, we have to first live that truth ourselves.

Confession: I feel most pressured by men of colour not to date outside my race.

As I walked through the streets of my suburb, I kissed my husband goodbye before we parted ways for the day. It was one of those typical hot and sunny summer Saturdays where you want to be outside but pay the price when the clothes you are wearing stick to your melting skin after just thirty minutes. As I turned away from Alex, I saw a dark-skinned Black man staring at us from further down the road. Nothing unusual. Stares do not phase me any more. I am in an interracial relationship, so they come with the territory. I am used to it.

My husband waved goodbye and ran for the coming train, but I decided to walk. I wiped the sweat from my forehead with the inside of my T-shirt. It was hot, so I had no shame. I then rummaged in my bag for a little fan to help me survive the blistering heat.

As I walked towards the man, I noticed he had a scowl on his face and I got a funny feeling, the kind you get when you know something bad is going to happen but you want to pretend it is all in your head.

That Black guy is looking at me after I kissed Alex, I started thinking. *I know that look . . . Maybe if I cross the street he'll let it go.* After crossing the road, I stole a peek over my shoulder. *Shit,* I said to myself, *he's still following me – this isn't going to end well.* It might sound like I was paranoid – I mean, how can someone tell what another person is going to do just from the look on their face? But I knew something was going to happen because I have experienced it before. I knew what the disapproving look meant, and the sucking of teeth and shaking of the head. Sometimes I have heard people shout 'Stick with your own!', but typically people keep walking, muttering indistinguishable comments under their breath.

As I quickened my pace, I started to turn my head to see if the man was still following me, and before I could even turn fully turn round, a big loogie landed on my neck. Yes, that's right. He *spat* on me. I froze, stunned. What the hell just happened? I had never been spat on before. Of all the names I have been called, and the aggressions I have experienced as a Black woman, I now know being spat on is the worst. It made me feel dirty. It made me feel like I was less than nothing.

Spitting is the most effective and universal way of saying 'fuck you' to someone without having to utter a word. After a few numbing seconds of trying to compute what had just happened, I wiped the spit off the side of my neck and grew hot with anger. And I knew that I couldn't do what I really wanted to.

You know that feeling when you want to punch someone in the face who clearly deserves it but can't because you know what'll happen? Honestly, and quite embarrassingly, the only thing holding me back from decking this man was the fear of jail. As I ran after him screaming, he glanced over his shoulder, while smirking at my visceral tantrum in the street.

He knew there was nothing I could really do, and he knew I knew it too. A young White guy standing nearby saw what happened. I never caught his name, but he looked like a Frank so let's call him that. Frank ran up to me and asked, 'Do you need any help?' and

I nodded vigorously pointing at the spitter fading into the distance.

A White guy is literally coming to my rescue to try to save me from something a Black man did to me. There's something very sad about this picture, I thought. Together, Frank and I ran after the man, who was calmly walking down the street.

I caught his eye when he momentarily looked back, and he picked up the pace. For someone who gave the illusion that he didn't care, he suddenly seemed nervous. 'Uh, quick question.' Frank turned to me, a little out of breath. 'What are we going to do when we actually catch up with this guy?'

Damn it, I thought. *I guess Frank isn't willing to punch him either.* 'Good question,' I said. 'Let's take a picture and send it to the police.' But by the time we had caught up with Mr Spit and Run, he had ducked into a nearby train. I looked at the train pulling away, feeling helpless and raw.

And that was it. I turned to Frank and thanked him for trying to help. 'Sorry that happened to you,' he whispered, and then he walked away.

On my way home, as I went over what had just happened, I realised that Mr Spit and Run only thought it was worth hiding and running when he saw that a

White man was involved – not when it was just me on my own. The race of the person he couldn't stand to see me kissing was the very race he seemed to be afraid of.

I never thought someone would do that to me, let alone someone from the Black community. I always assumed that prejudice would only come from White people, as I grew up being taught that they were the only ones who cause minorities to feel oppressed and marginalised.

To this stranger I did not belong. I was a traitor to my own race and deserved to be punished. While it was wrong what he did, I can perhaps imagine how he felt. In a world where he has likely been through hardships based on the colour of his skin, and probably experienced daily aggressions and racism at the hands of White people, it could have been very hard for him to see a Black woman show affection to someone from a race that has caused him to hurt. That's what racism does to people who are on the receiving end. It hurts, degrades and can create a sort of anger and bitterness that is very hard to ignore.

Confession: I know very well that my husband is White, so it is annoying when people remind me.

My husband and I met on a journalism master's course in London. It was an international course that lasted one year and brought together a fascinating cast of characters from all over the world. Established journalists from Spain, Pakistan, India and South Africa were there, alongside students from Somalia, the Lebanon, Syria, Australia, Germany, Holland and the USA, among others.

After a month or so of being on the course, I bumped into Alex on campus. We had seen each other in lectures but hadn't really chatted. Alex came up to me and said, 'Hello . . . Tameka right?' I politely but abruptly corrected him. 'It's Tineka,' and went on my way. My husband's recollection of that encounter involves plenty more tension and attitude. I don't think it was that dramatic, but I do remember at the time being annoyed that so many people in Britain couldn't pronounce my name. It's pronounced TAH-NEE-KA not TAN-E-KA – and certainly not TAM-E-KA. I'm not very good at hiding my emotions, so perhaps I *was* a bit rude on that day.

Alex later told me he was shocked by my confidence and direct manner towards a stranger, and, in fact, was offended by our first meeting. However, after he showed up to my birthday party with a mutual friend and I greeted him with open arms – I'd had a few glasses of wine by then – he thought I was an all right person.

Our friendship really blossomed the following semester when, with my usual directness, I offered Alex some friendly advice about what our coursemates thought of him. He spotted me in a study room and came in to say hello. We were chatting about what we were planning on doing that weekend and I mentioned a couple of different parties I planned on attending, at which point Alex realised he wasn't invited to any of them.

'Oh, wow, I'm really out of the loop,' he said.

I leant in and put my hand on his shoulder. 'Listen, I'm going to tell you something, and I think you should take my advice.'

Alex started to chuckle. 'Oh no, I'm afraid what you're going to say!'

'No. No, it's nothing bad, just something to think about,' I responded. 'Listen, I think you're a really cool guy. *But* you always sit in the front row of the class.

And, no offence, but you always ask questions that require a twenty-minute answer ten minutes before the class ends,' I said. 'So every time you raise your hand, we all roll our eyes because we know the class will run over. So how about this?' I said. 'Sit a few rows back and on the side. And if you have a question, ask it thirty minutes before the end of class. And then see whether you start to be invited to parties.'

And the very next day in class I saw him sit several rows back and he asked his questions well before the end of the class. Fast-forward a few months and he was invited to more parties, and I always made sure he was included in any events.

At this point in time Alex had a long-term girlfriend. We didn't speak about her much but would often hang out with friends together and alone sometimes. By the time the course ended we had become very good friends and decided to move into an apartment along with a couple of other friends – a White American girl from California and a mixed-race American woman from Virginia.

A few months after moving in, Alex's relationship ended, and we gradually developed feelings for each other. But this was complicated because we lived together, and friends do not always make good lovers.

During a friend's birthday party we impulsively kissed each other in secret and kept it from our friends and family for several months.

The fact that we had different skin colour was never an issue or a topic of conversation when we first started dating.

When I was in Alabama for Christmas, I visited my grandma at her home. After standing around in the kitchen for some time, dodging various questions about my love life, I finally confessed that I was dating someone in the UK.

'What is he?' my grandma asked.

'He's British,' I said.

'OK. What is he?' she asked again.

'He's British,' I said again.

'But *what* is he?' she asked a third time.

'He's British,' I replied a third time.

Finally my grandma asked outright, 'Is he White?'

'Yes,' I said.

She paused a bit, nodding her head in slow motion and replied, 'OK', her poker face giving nothing away.

One of my aunts then asked, 'Does he have a sexy British accent?'

'Uh, sure,' I said, laughing awkwardly and glancing around the room for an excuse to make an exit. 'I need to use the bathroom,' I announced loudly as I left the room in a hurry.

By the time I returned to the kitchen the conversation had moved on. *I survived,* I thought. I found a place round the kitchen table and listened to my family gossip about their friends and other family members – grateful it wasn't me for the time being.

Before Alex had met any of my family, he overheard a conversation with one of my closest relatives. I was on the phone with my cousin when she informed me that she had heard some gossip about the mysterious man I was dating.

'So, I heard about your friend,' she said. It was a matter-of-fact statement followed by a pause and then a long 'hmmmmm'. 'I'm gonna have to feel his *vibe*.'

My cousin is one of the few people I know in the world who is naturally kind, and has always been protective of me. But she was on speakerphone and Alex overheard what sounded to him like a threat – someone he would have to work hard to impress.

By the time I took him to meet my family in the USA he was frightened. It was Christmastime and we were engaged, so he hoped that factor would account for his *vibe* plenty. Alex had got down on one knee and presented a ring six months earlier, during a holiday in southern France. I had balled my eyes out and said yes through sobs.

Americans have a sort of fascination with the British – accents and all. And I really saw this in my family's interactions with Alex. My mother's family fell for Alex hook, line and sinker. I was shocked because they are not easy to please. In fact, they ignored me the entire time, giving in to Alex's every whim, feeding him copious amounts of food and taking him anywhere he wanted to go on his first trip to the USA.

The next stop on the trip was to Alabama to introduce him to my dad's side of the family. Alex had a lot of trouble with Southern accents, so he would always sit next to me and turn to me when he couldn't understand what my dad or other family members were saying. When visiting with my sisters, grandmom and grandpop, my grandma was finally able to see with her own eyes that Alex really was, in fact, White. She greeted him warmly and insisted on holding hands and praying in a circle before we left, which greatly amused Alex.

We quickly realised that my family was much more interested in Alex being British than him being White. With my family the colour of his skin never came up in conversation – although that wasn't true elsewhere.

His nationality, however, was talked about with wide-eyed fascination, curiosity, confusion and intrigue.

One morning, my dad took us out for breakfast at a pancake place outside Birmingham, Alabama. The establishment was not high-end by any means, but the food was good, and the service was quick and friendly.

'What can I get y'all?' asked a young Black waitress when she approached our table. Her eyes were down as she took a notepad out of her pocket. When she looked up and saw us ready to order, her head snapped back and she failed to hide her confusion. It was plain to read on her face: *Why is this White dude sitting at this table with a Black family? How does he fit in?*

After the long pause and stare, we finally ordered and had a great time. That was the first time Alex had really felt out of place on that trip. The restaurant was filled with mostly minorities, which of course didn't bother Alex. It was being stared at that did. But honestly, I think this was an important experience for him, because it's sometimes how I feel in all-White situations.

He later said to me that the most significant part of that diner experience was that the White and Black people were sitting in different parts of the restaurant. To be honest I hadn't really noticed but for him it was shocking. I don't know if that was the restaurant seating customers of different races in different sections, but in this day and age why is that still happening? Perhaps it's for the very same reason I didn't notice it. When I'm in the South I resign myself to thinking things are a certain way and act accordingly to avoid trouble. I imagine people of all races, colours and cultures unwittingly do the same thing. But by doing this we're allowing ourselves to be a cog in the machine of racial separation and discrimination. So I guess even *I* have blinders that I need to become more aware of.

While I thankfully didn't have to worry about family issues with Alex, I did with friends, and that was a surprise for me. Some of my friends didn't hide the fact that they weren't thrilled about me dating a White man. These friends were often men of colour, which sometimes caused me to question my friendships with them when it came to their views on interracial dating. Sometimes they were a bit close to the bone, but generally speaking what really bothered me was the need for them to lecture me on dating men outside my race – and in public conversation.

I would awkwardly dodge the questions or sheepishly shake my head and laugh them off. 'How come I have never seen you date Black men?' one of them asked during a conversation with a group of friends. 'Because they never ask me out,' I replied. This was, of course, after my friends had discovered I had started dating the man who would become my husband. 'How did this happen?' some of them asked. 'Were you drunk?'

Some of these men have gone on to have serious relationships with White women.

This situation is not uncommon. There are countless men of colour who judge women of colour dating outside their race, only to shamelessly do the same themselves. I believe that even within racial communities, gender expectations and stereotypes make it harder for women to date outside their race – while many men are able to do so with much less ridicule.

Take, for example, my White sister-in law who dates outside her race, only for Black women to yell at her on the street, 'Stop stealing our men!' This is the truth of being in an interracial relationship.

It is the one type of relationship where people are not only judged on their own skin colour, but the skin colour of their significant other. Now that is what some might call a truly beleaguered union.

4

RACISM 101: CLASS IS NOW IN SESSION

TINEKA

Confession: When my White friends open up to me about their views on race, it's not awesome.

I feel a little guilty talking about this confession. Because I'm married to a White man, I feel some sort of obligation to hear my White friends out when they voice their opinions on race – most of the time containing bias or racist rhetoric. I don't know why I feel this way – I guess it's because I think they expect me to have more of an understanding from their point of view because I am with someone who is White. We often learn intimate insights about our partner's family, friends, upbringing, culture and race, so perhaps in a way this assumption does make sense.

In my experience, many White Europeans have a contrived idea that racism is not a serious problem in Europe. I think this is linked to the fact that many want to forget Europe's leading role in the slave trade, while happily pointing the finger at the abhorrent behaviour openly practised in the American South, its remnants still seen and felt today in the USA. However, just because the history of slavery and racism within Europe is not as obvious – if one can even describe it as such – doesn't make it any less sinister. When talking about race with European friends, acquaintances or even colleagues, it is not uncommon for me to hear something along the lines of, 'Oh, but that's just America. Racism isn't really a big thing here in Europe.' Just because something is more hidden, doesn't make it any less dangerous. In my experience it is still ever present, and in ways more frustrating, as 'diet racism', also known as racial microaggressions, can be harder to address than overt racism. I've come to realise that the power of microaggressions lie in their subtlety. This makes it almost impossible for minorities to pinpoint or call out their attackers.

I begrudgingly feel I have a responsibility not to get angry, to be understanding when several people of an entirely different race tell me it's OK that the White actor Joseph Fiennes played Michael Jackson in an episode of the Sky Arts series *Urban Myths*, because, after all, Michael Jackson had surgery to *look* White and if it's a comedy, then that's fine. They then state that, besides, it was Michael Jackson himself who said, 'It don't matter if you're black or white.' In the end,

Sky did not even broadcast the episode due to public backlash.

I have to watch their eyes glaze over and their ears close when I explain that their argument is the same as many other White people, including Joseph Fiennes himself. And that Michael Jackson actually had vitiligo, a skin disease that affects all races but is most noticeable in Black women and men, where white patches appear on the skin. I never really understood why some casting directors think that they can get away with placing White actors in Black roles, especially in historical depictions. But then in 2019 the biopic about Harriet Tubman – the African-American slave who formed the Underground Railroad that lead countless slaves to freedom – titled *Harriet,* was released to rave reviews. Shortly after the film's release, news broke that the script had actually picked up interest from a studio in 1994. However, a movie studio executive had wanted to cast Julia Roberts in the role of Harriet Tubman. They wanted to cast a White woman with red hair as a dark-skinned Black slave. If that doesn't show the institutional racism that is still rife within society, I don't know what else does. When the studio executive was told by the only Black person in the room that Harriet Tubman was, in fact, a Black woman – his response was 'that was so long ago, no one will know that'. I feel comments like these really encompass the problem that many White people don't understand the viewpoints or feelings of minorities. They haven't had to suffer racism, and being enslaved is not a part of their history. There seems to be a dire lack of empathy. To say that no one will notice a White person playing the role of arguably the most prominent Black hero during slavery is appalling, and it shows a complete disconnect from reality. It shows a lack of understanding that Black people still suffer from generations of slavery and their ancestors being enslaved.

I see their rolling eyes when I insist there are numerous light-skinned and even 'White-passing' Black actors who could have played the role of Michael Jackson, that it's important that one of the most talented Black pop icons of our time should always be represented by a Black man, since Black people receive so few nods for their contributions and work as it is.

I had to hold back my shock at the racial and historical ignorance of a colleague confidently saying in a conversation with a laugh that Barack Obama, a trailblazer and hero to the Black community, should be *grateful* to the slave trade, as he would have never become president of the United States without it. Or listen in horror when a friend openly admitted that if she was walking down a street at night and saw a group of Black people on the corner, she would most certainly cross the street for her own safety.

Recently, my husband and I were eating dinner with two other friends when I was asked about the work I do with different international organisations. I often have a flexible work schedule (and I will usually negotiate it before taking on a project), which allows me the time I need to also manage our greetings-card business, Huetribe. Alex and I started Huetribe because of the lack of diverse representation on UK greetings cards. Our cards feature people of different races and sexualities. We first created it because we could never find cards for our anniversaries, and realised that there are thousands of people globally who have the same problem. We also talk to retailers large and small about the importance of offering their customers cards for people of all backgrounds. Unfortunately, some UK retailers believe that cards that feature anyone who is not White are too 'niche', and some retailers have claimed 'The UK isn't ready for that yet', but we're very passionate about making a change in this area, and are slowly starting to see some impact – one greetings card at a time.

After listening for a few minutes, one friend – who is White, male and British – informed me that I am 'lazy' and lacking a 'work ethic'. I was stunned, as the comment came out of nowhere. 'Umm, excuse me?' I said.

'You don't have any work ethic and you don't know what hard work is,' my friend elaborated.

'I prefer to work smarter not harder,' I retorted. 'If I focus, I can finish eight hours of work in four to five hours by not taking coffee breaks every fifteen minutes or sitting in long meetings.'

'I don't care. You not wanting to work a full day is pure laziness,' he responded.

At this point my voice started to rise. I have a serious issue when someone tries to diminish my accomplishments or, worse, calls me lazy. I had to work hard to build my career to the point where I can choose my work hours and what I do. 'As a Black woman, I've had to overcome obstacles that most people are oblivious to. I've led teams at the United Nations, advised senior directors and I have my own business. And I had to do it all without the help of being a White male,' I retaliated.

'I don't need you to list out your CV for me,' he responded.

I was shocked. 'You have no idea how offensive you calling me lazy is – as a Black woman, I have to work twice as hard, longer hours and if I even make *one* mistake, it follows me. I don't think I could have gotten to where I am today by being lazy.'

I looked over at our White female friend, who was silently sitting across the table. I then turned to my husband. I know he has an aversion to confrontation, but still I hoped that he would come to my defence. 'Alex, don't I have a strong work ethic?'

'Well, I never worked with you before,' he responded. My mouth dropped in shock. He knew the long hours I worked and every detail of my various jobs. Not to mention the fact that we have a business together – which I manage.

I felt betrayed. I was surrounded by three White people. One attacking my career and work ethic for no reason, the other after having been silent for the entire conversation only speaking up to tell me to calm down, and my husband failing to come to my defence.

'Why isn't anyone telling him to stop attacking me?!' I cried.

Finally, Alex said to our friend, 'You're being a bit harsh.'

'A BIT?!' I exclaimed.

Then my friend, who had started this whole mess, said something I will never forget. 'What's wrong with you, Tineka? What happened to you? You're talking so much about race. I feel sorry and concerned thinking that you two will have mixed-race children one day.'

I'm pretty sure my head spun round a few times and, before I could react, Alex jumped in and told our friend his comment was inappropriate.

Situations like these make me feel like a cornered animal. I was the only Black woman in the room and I felt I was being attacked.

I felt railroaded. Maybe my friend was having a bad day. Perhaps he wasn't happy with his own career and felt the need to criticise someone else. But why did he feel the need to mention teaching any children we might have about race? As if it would be some horrific thing? Whatever the reason, it made me feel like shit. And why did he feel sorry for any children we might have? Because I will teach them about racism? Perhaps he had a misguided view that I would be giving any future children a complex about race by forcing them to worry about it. But that very statement showed his White privilege. Because it is a position of privilege for him to think that a person should not need to teach their children about race – and that is because he never had to experience racism.

This conversation reminded me of a horrible moment in my career working at a major PR firm in London: sitting at a table being yelled at by a White man who didn't like my ambition or entitlement to be proud of the work I had accomplished in my career. I joined the team and was quickly promoted, mainly thanks to my background in journalism. The only other person on the team with a similar background was my manager, a White male in a senior position. It was during this time I learnt that having a White male on your side – not just in the workplace but also in any situation – was golden. Sad but true. I learnt about White *and* male privilege – and that having someone on your side really influences others with those same privileges. The term 'White privilege' became better known after the release of a 1988 paper called *White Privilege and Male Privilege: A Personal Account of Coming to See Correspondences Through Work in Women's Studies* by Dr Peggy McIntosh. McIntosh described White privilege as an invisible package of unearned assets that she can count on cashing in each day, but about which she was 'meant' to remain oblivious. According to McIntosh, White privilege is like an invisible weightless knapsack of special provisions, assurances, tools, maps, guides, codebooks, passports, visas, clothes, compasses, emergency gear and blank cheques.

She compared this to male privilege in the sense that 'rarely will a man go beyond acknowledging that women are disadvantaged to acknowledging that men have unearned advantage, or that unearned privilege has not been good for men's development as human beings, or for society's development, or that privilege systems might ever be challenged and changed.'

Most poignantly, Dr McIntosh lists in her paper all the privileges she has come to realise she and other White people benefit from in daily life. Some of which she states:

> 'I can go home from most meetings of organisations I belong to feeling somewhat tied in, rather than isolated, out of place, outnumbered, unheard, held at a distance or feared.
>
> 'I can be pretty sure that an argument with a colleague of another race is more likely to jeopard-

> ise her chances for advancement than to jeopardise mine.
>
> 'If I declare there is a racial issue at hand, or there isn't a racial issue at hand, my race will lend me more credibility for either position than a person of colour will have.'[8]

Of all the privileges just mentioned, I have benefited from them only because I had a White manager that fully supported me and my ambitions. So when I was forced to change managers I lost that golden protection – and I knew it. I begged the managing director of the team to allow me to stay with my current one. He told me, 'Frankly, Tineka, it's not up to you.' I was then put on one of the biggest and most prestigious projects in the team, and a senior colleague – who thought he should have my position on the project instead – constantly attacked me. He asked me to always email before approaching his desk. This was not a requirement for any of our White colleagues. When I was overloaded with tasks, I became sick and had to take some time off. The senior colleague threatened me and said that my reputation would be 'purposely' ruined if it happened again. I didn't know what I had done wrong.

I then discovered that my White male colleagues with considerably less experience were getting paid more than me. We had an almost equal number of men and women on our team. Yet the women stayed in junior roles or took twice as long as the men to move up in seniority. When I asked for a raise during one meeting, I was ripped to shreds and told to 'know my place' and that my ambition was blinding me. I did not know about racial microaggressions then or the misogynoir that is directed towards Black women where race and gender both play roles in bias. I knew I was treated differently because of my race, but I had no way to define the treatment and I had no other minorities on the team to confide in. I sat in a glass room with my new manager and watched as he balled his fist in anger as I asked for a raise and promotion. I had outlined my accomplishments and made clear that they were at the level I was asking to be promoted to. I had used the same method with my previous manager – in fact, it was his idea – and it had worked well. Why was it a problem now?

My new manager began to swear at me and say what a horrible person I was, how I would probably climb over my friends at work (who were all White) to move up the corporate ladder. This was the first time I ever had anyone speak to me in that way. Given that I was the only minority in our department, and that another White male colleague was asking for the exact same thing at the same time, I knew he was talking to me like this because I was Black and probably because of my gender too. My supervisor sat on the department board and had a say in approving promotions and raises. He had approved someone less qualified than me but became volatile when I asked for the same treatment. If I were a White man, would my manager have admired my ambition? I believe so. There were many White men in that team who were just as or more ambitious than me. They were rewarded for it and I was reprimanded.

The realisation of this, the screaming, his body motioning as if he was about to hit me and his fist pounding the table to make a point, made me begin to sob – I was bawling. Tears, snot and gulps ensued. And there was not one ounce of sympathy from him. All this took place in a glass room, and I wondered, *How can no one see what is happening in this room?* Or worse, they see what is happening and they don't care. I felt so isolated. When I subsequently decided to resign and leave the company, I was met with even more hostility because many believed I owed them, that 'I'd be nowhere if it wasn't for them', and that they had a claim to me.

I always like to point out that 'some' not 'all' White people behave in this manner. I did have many White colleagues of all levels, including managers and senior directors, come up to me and tell me they thought the way I was being treated for leaving was shocking and wrong. And I appreciated that. It was just a shame none of them felt the need to report the behaviour to HR.

The dinnertime attack with friends gave me flashbacks to this moment: the aggression from another White male about work accomplishments and confidence in the value of my work. After the dinner, I explained to Alex why it's important for him to support me in situations like these, whether he likes confrontation or not. I pointed out that, as a couple, we should always support each other if one of us is being attacked. After we had spoken, Alex waited a few days and then he called our friend and explained just how hurt I had been. Our friend apologised to my husband for the things he said to me and mentioned he didn't know that many Black people go through these issues every day. The sad thing was that he couldn't even say sorry to me. He felt that apologising to his fellow White male friend was good enough.

And in altercations like these I am sad to say that I doubt my husband. I do not know if I can depend on him in racially tense discussions. It's also not my job to educate White people about racism and prejudice. But if I can have an impact on just one person, then I am satisfied. So I grit my teeth, try to avoid being offensive and often refer to real-life scenarios. Every now and again a friend says something that shows they've learnt, their view has changed or they openly admit they have a new perspective on racial issues and that some of their views were wrong. It is hard. It is soul-crushing. But I guess it's worth it. Right?

Alex and I are happily married but that doesn't mean we don't have differences of opinion. Sometimes even Alex unintentionally makes assumptions about me that he might not if my skin colour was different. If a crime had just occurred and a suspect is yet to be seen or found, would you think a seventy-five-year-old White lady was the culprit or the twenty-seven-year-old Black woman? Or in a public argument it's easy to think the person of colour is the aggressor rather than the sweet-looking White woman. On one occasion we were on holiday in Switzerland and had to take a train to get back to our home in Geneva. Swiss trains are super clean, comfortable and punctual. Sometimes the train journeys in Switzerland feel like part of the holiday. I love travelling by train in Switzerland, so I was really looking forward to relaxing.

Alex and I sat in a four-seater section and decided to sit diagonally across from each other to give the other more room for the journey. As I had some extra room, I decided to cross my legs. Now, my legs are quite long, and the tip of my shoe came close to the seat in front of me. But by no means was my shoe actually touching the seat in front of me. We had been sitting for about ten minutes when a White woman in her seventies stood up from her seat across the aisle and approached me.

'Excuse me,' she said.

'Yes?' I said in response.

She leant down, placed her hands on her knees and put her face very close to mine. I suddenly felt as if I was back in preschool, being told off by one of my teachers. 'Do you put your dirty little feet on the furniture at *your* house?'

I was in shock. 'Are you talking to me?' I asked turning my head to look around in disbelief, certain she was talking to someone else.

'Yes, you should know better than to put your dirty feet on the seat in front of you.' She went on.

I tried to maintain my calm. I glanced down the aisle. I was the only person of colour sitting in the train car. I could spot at least three other people with their legs crossed in the same position as me with their feet close to the chair in front of them in a similar fashion. They were all White.

'First of all, my feet aren't on the seat. Second of all, it's pathetic that you have to come across the aisle to bother me when I'm doing nothing to you or the seat in front of me. You haven't approached anyone else in this car and yet there are several other people sitting in the same position as me. Why is that?'

'Don't get so defensive,' she said.

Now, I'd like to take a pause in this story to say I HATE THIS PHRASE. Every time I have experienced a White person saying something racist or displaying microaggressions, as soon as I defend myself or question them about their statement, the immediate response is 'Don't get so defensive'. I am always tempted to say, 'Then don't be so racist.' I have been in many situations where White friends or colleagues struggle to realise that they themselves can say racist things. And as soon as I point it out, their response makes me feel like the angry Black woman who always plays the race card.

So as this woman said the phrase I dread the most, I held my composure because, as my dad taught me, if I, the only Black person on the train had an outburst, people will likely think I'm the crazy one harassing the sweet elderly White lady. And, hey, if I was on the outside looking in, I might think the same thing too – we all have issues with bias.

'I don't want you to be offended,' she continued.

'Then leave me alone,' I said to the woman. 'Go back to your seat and find something to occupy yourself.'

But she would not go away and we continued to argue. At this point I looked at Alex, who was watching silently. I looked at him with a pleading expression on my face. The woman had clearly assumed we were not together, and she followed my gaze and looked at him in confusion. And at that moment he disappointed me. He looked at me in frustration then abruptly and sharply turned his head and his body the other way to stare out of the window. He pretended he didn't even know me.

I was so hurt by his reaction I just stopped talking.

I felt crushed by it and didn't have the desire to fight any more. The woman noticed something was going on between us at that point and walked away.

When we got home, I told Alex I couldn't believe his reaction and he told me that I was the one who behaved inappropriately.

'You were arguing with an old lady, Tineka. That was out of line,' he responded curtly.

'Are you kidding me?! I was literally staring out of the window when that woman came up to me and attacked me for being Black and sitting! She targeted me because I am Black,' I continued. 'How do I know that? Because most of the people in our carriage sat the same way. And she talked to me like I was dumb and had no manners or house training. It was humiliating.'

'Tineka, you shouldn't care. She was an old lady who doesn't know any better,' Alex said.

'Age is no excuse for the mistreatment of others,' I clapped back. 'Your White privilege blinds you to a lot of things, but now I can't even trust that you'll have my back. Plus I can't believe you pretended not to even know me,' I responded.

Our argument continued for days. One evening we had two Black female friends over and we told them what had happened.

'Uh, yeah, Alex, she definitely was treating Tineka differently. It's super obvious – how would you not understand that? Duh!' one of our friends replied.

'Really?' Alex said. 'I honestly don't see how you could make that assumption.'

And this is the nub of the issue when it comes to mixed-race families or minority friends sharing their experiences of racism with White people. There is such a disregard at times for taking us at our word, even if *we* are the ones who live it every day. How can a race of people try to tell another race that their experience isn't valid or argue against it if they have *no idea* what it's like to walk in their shoes and the world has been made essentially for someone like them? It's in instances like these that I see how blinding Alex's privilege can be, and it's so hard to get through.

ALEX

From my point of view it was annoying that the woman decided to tell Tineka her opinion about hygiene and etiquette on trains, but I didn't recognise the exchange as a racially motivated attack. For me this elderly woman was simply being old-fashioned, and if she came off as being condescending, then that was a shame but nothing to get so upset about. It's hard for me to say exactly *why* I think that way, but I can certainly say that was my gut reaction. I wonder now whether it is partly because I am a White man who doesn't experience these kinds of comments as regularly as Tineka does. And, of course, my preference towards avoiding conflict is partly a result of that. When I was witnessing this exchange, I thought that it was unnecessary for the lady to have intervened and also unnecessary for Tineka to react so strongly.

I like to think that if I were put in the same situation, I would have been annoyed at the woman but kept those feelings to myself and simply reacted calmly. I am confident I would have taken a more pragmatic approach and avoided an argument. I would have removed my feet from the vicinity of the chair opposite, placed them firmly on the floor of the train for a few minutes to satisfy her, and then quietly returned to the sitting position that I find most comfortable. At the time this happened I didn't think it was worth trying to teach the woman a lesson, to remind her that she should mind her own business and just move along.

I would also say that how I interpreted the event was influenced by the woman's age; I saw someone older with old-fashioned views and I didn't want to be the person who doesn't listen to another generation. It took a long time and many conversations before I even started to appreciate the reality: we were both there but saw different things, different layers. I do accept that it is remarkable that I interpreted this event so very differently to Tineka. I still don't know for sure whether or not it was a racial attack.

Let's say we randomly bumped into that woman again and asked her straight up what motivated her to talk to Tineka in that way, and she in turn answered honestly. I don't think she would say it was about race. But does that mean that it wasn't? Or was she acting out of a more subtle, almost subconscious bias?

Now that I can look back at that encounter and mull over the conversations it sparked between Tineka and me, it is very clear that I am better off because of it. What I know now is that it is up to me to take the mental leap, change my thinking and simply accept that the way I interpreted the situation was influenced by the fact that I am a White man who gets treated very differently in similar situations. When people I don't know talk to me, they don't address me in a way that shows they know better and have something to teach me. Sometimes people make suggestions or recommendations, but they don't instruct me. And that is because people are biased and live with assumptions built into their thinking. My understanding of who I am is partly shaped by the assumptions others bring out during interactions with me, and I feel good about myself and how I behave on trains, in shops, during professional meetings and in public settings. I feel good about myself because people don't tell me off or instruct me to correct the way I am sitting, the way I talk or the way I interact with others. I am confident I am doing things right because nobody tells me otherwise.

And only in the rare cases where I am witness to the way Tineka is treated do I get a sense of how different my experience is. It is a clash of understanding and a clash of cultures. Our life experiences happen in the same physical spaces, but we are living very different experiences. There is also another important element in this learning: trust. It is easy for me to forget that this inequality is not new to Tineka. She has lived her whole life with different expectations as to how others behave and has constantly been comparing her experiences to those she sees White people receive. She has a perspective I can't catch up with because she has years of experience that I don't have. This means it's up to me to give her perspective real credibility in my mind, even if I don't agree or share her point of view. It's a leap of faith that doesn't come naturally to me because I haven't gone through the same learning. It's important I become more familiar with her perspective and more comfortable accepting what I don't know as, ultimately, we're stronger as a couple if we challenge each other but land in the same vicinity.

5

BEING IN AN INTERRACIAL MARRIAGE DOES NOT MAKE A WHITE MAN WOKE

ALEX

'Don't act like you are all woke now, Alex. Just because you're married to me doesn't mean you're entitled to get all upset when your Black colleagues say something you think is racially wrong.'

When those words came rushing out of Tineka's mouth one evening, they hurt. The words were a warning, but it felt like I was being scolded. It wasn't what I had wanted to hear or expected to hear from the person I trust the most in the world. This scathing admonishment was Tineka's gut response after I told her in great depth about a challenging and painful set of racially charged moments I had witnessed, and maybe even been involved in. I was already shaken up and confused by what I had witnessed and thought that by talking it through with Tineka I could process what I had seen, take stock and recalibrate things. Instead, Tineka threw a spanner into my thinking. Was I not able to perceive racism and other social issues as well as I thought I could? Was I not woke? It was some White-man self-doubt compounded by miscommunication, and I was left speechless.

Here are the events I described to Tineka:

Not long ago, I worked a desk job in a European city, and the office I worked in was a very multicultural place. There were people from Germany, Kenya, USA, Switzerland, Canada, Sweden, Venezuela – well, pretty much everywhere. We worked on media campaigns and the work was interesting most of the time and the colleagues were a good bunch of people.

After I had worked there for a few months, I met a colleague who was normally based in one of the organisation's locations in Africa. He was a larger-than-life American guy, probably in his early forties, and he was Black. Before I actually met him, I had heard about his work and how he was well respected for working hard and helping younger colleagues with less experience. Everyone told me he was a team player. When we met, it was a chance encounter near my desk on a hot afternoon and we got chatting about work stuff. This colleague told me he had heard we were probably going to work together on some campaigns.

He was friendly and we got chatting about more personal things. He asked me where I was from and whether I was married. I told him that I was from London and had moved to Switzerland with my wife and I explained that my wife was American. He asked me more about my wife, including where she was from in the States, and I replied factually: her mum is from New Jersey and her dad is from Alabama. She grew up all along the East Coast. Then he asked me a few questions that changed the atmosphere and made me feel uncomfortable.

'What is your wife's name?'

'Tineka,' I replied, starting to wonder where this line of enquiry was going.

Then he told me he was going to ask me something straight up. 'Is your wife Black?'

I was stunned by such a direct and kind of rude question. I like to think of myself as a professional person. I am also polite and British, sometimes very guarded. Especially so when I am in a professional context.

'Ummm, yeah,' I replied.

I turned back to my computer, signalling that the chat was over. I opened my inbox and pretended to be busy. But as I sat there and stared at the screen, two questions lingered in my mind:

1. Did I respond to that question correctly or should I have responded by telling him I didn't want to answer the question?

2. Why is that such a different kind of question to 'Where did you meet your wife?' or 'Does your wife like skiing?' – those kinds of chit-chat questions?

This question about my wife's skin colour certainly *felt* different to me, and I think it hit me hard because nobody else had ever asked me that. At that point Tineka and I had been together slightly over four years, and nobody else had felt the need to query whether I was with a Black person or a White person.

The line of interrogation about my private life had gone too far – I didn't want to talk about the colour of my wife's skin. I didn't suspect that the question had come from a nasty or mean place, and I might have even detected some excitement in the way he had asked, like he wanted to connect with other Black people in this predominantly White town that was far from his home. My colleague didn't seem to be thinking badly of me for marrying a Black person, and he wasn't overtly criticising my wife for marrying a White person. But it felt to me like he had pushed the boundary and asked a question that was too probing and bordering on judgemental. I wondered if he was asking me about Tineka's skin colour because he wanted to assign me and my wife a specific place in his thinking and make assumptions about us as a mixed-race couple, and whatever that flagged in his own mind and experience. From my perspective this conversation was going down a racial path and into territory that I did not want to explore. Maybe I was being an awkward White guy, but I didn't feel good after that conversation and being put in that position. There were so many things we could have casually chatted about, all the way from work, politics and travel to family and our views on TV shows. Why did it have to come to Black or White?

Over the years that followed, I worked closely with this guy. We had similar professional interests and we both got a kick out of applying ourselves and working on creative projects. He was smart and I learnt a lot from him. And I valued his support as I grew within the organisation because he would recommend other teams trust me with interesting projects. I put the previous incident to the back of my mind, and learnt that overall he was a decent man. But then something else happened.

We worked together on a project with another colleague, who happened to be a Black woman. I knew her skills, what she could bring to the project to make it a success and I also had an idea of her level of professionalism in the office. So, the project team was three people: me, a White male, and two Black colleagues, one male and one female. There was no hierarchy within the team; we all had to contribute and the difference in our skin colours or backgrounds was not part of the project and did not define how we were to work together. We were a team of three professionals who had to deliver a certain campaign on deadline. When I say it like that, it all sounds so clear and simple.

The project went smoothly at first and then one of my colleagues made a small error. It was the kind of mistake that anybody could have made. It just so happened that the person who made the mistake was a Black woman and the person who had spotted the mistake was a White man. No biggie, just something that needed to be corrected. Our roles could have easily been reversed so I did not make a big deal out of it.

The colleague who had made the error left the office to go and fix the problem, and at that point the other team member came over to me. It was the colleague who had previously asked if Tineka was Black, and this time he was shaking his head. Then he quietly muttered a rhetorical question. 'Why is it always easier working with White guys than Black women?'

I was the only person who had heard his words and I felt put on the spot – shocked, embarrassed, confused. Another unnecessary racial comment had entered the workplace. A colleague had made an error, but that was not a reflection of who she was as a woman or as a Black woman. I was a little frustrated the error had happened but I did not feel any need to make the assumption that a person with White skin and straight hair could deliver the work better than anyone else.

I could not come up with a decent response on the spot, and that frustrated me further. Could I accuse him of being racist? But I knew how that would sound; just imagine, a younger White guy telling a more worldly Black man to stop with the racism. It would have sounded awful and condescending, right? It would have been turned round on me and I would have been accused of escalating things, making a mountain out of a molehill. If I had actually accused my Black colleague of being racist against Black people, I would have looked stupid. I would have ruined our friendship and severely damaged our professional relationship. I could have taken a more constructive approach and reminded him that it was just a small mistake that could be easily fixed. But he could have taken that response as me joining in the banter. The last thing I wanted to do was send a signal that I actually agreed with his perspective: White men are better to work with, such a shame we have to be all politically correct these days and endure these errors our Black female colleagues make. I was silent, and I think he realised I wasn't pleased with this awkward situation. But I didn't find the words; I didn't really defend the other colleague who was being judged and belittled. I look back on that moment and I am not proud of myself. Tineka had mentioned to me that negative comments Black people make about other Black people is a 'complicated problem within the Black community', one that I, as a White man, could never understand. It was only then that I realised what she meant.

For the rest of that day the episode played over in my head. I kept on approaching it like a puzzle that could somehow be solved. *Why* would it be helpful to make that kind of distinction? I did my own head in, going round and round in circles. We were just trying to get on with the work, dealing with a high-powered workplace and demanding colleagues. This is not an easy scenario for anybody to be in, irrespective of their skin colour. I couldn't talk to other colleagues either, because I didn't want to cause drama or make the situation any worse than it was. I didn't want to make it formal, but perhaps I should have done, and dealt with the fallout.

Through this thinking I came to a fairly obvious realisation – I had witnessed an event that happens a million times every day all over the world: a microaggression. A throwaway comment that was said unconsciously, yet a statement that speaks volumes about how racial discrimination and sexism are alive today. When high-profile politicians or celebrities are racist, they are subjected to hate on Twitter and in the media. But when things are said, or whispered, between people who know one another, this is a different scenario. It was up to me to take the tough call and make this man realise what he had said and just how painful it was. It was on me to say something, but I had stayed silent.

The whole episode made me reflect on how being in an interracial marriage has had an impact on how I perceive and think about situations like this. This episode also made me realise that many of the lessons I had learnt during my marriage to Tineka were actually sinking in, but I had somehow missed a very specific point. I am not proud to admit it, but the reality is that it had never really occurred to me that Black people would judge other Black people in this way. I had thought that racism was when White people treated people from other ethnic groups with contempt or disrespect – White people like me who do not even know how it feels to be discriminated against. I can't count the number of times I have seen my White friends and colleagues call other White people stupid, incompetent or ugly, but I've never heard them say that while also pointing out that they're White. I know that people aren't always patient, tolerant or forgiving, especially in tense situations where someone has failed to deliver what was expected of them, but I had never before witnessed that through a racial lens. I have never heard a White person actually express that they prefer working with a particular racial group. I know that must happen every day, but just not among my friends, family and colleagues, who are generally tolerant, open-minded people who appreciate and celebrate diversity.

Most days I get to the end of the workday, shut down my computer and make a conscious effort to leave all my work at the office. I don't like to bring any workplace drama home, and I prefer to keep a balance between work and home life. But on that day I had to speak to Tineka about what had gone on, get her take on the situation and start processing my reaction and letting the whole ugly thing go before I got angrier. I told myself that because Tineka is a Black person who has experienced racism, she would be interested in talking this over with her White husband.

I am married to someone who has the capacity to listen properly. Tineka can hear what I have to say and let me get to the end with mistakes and all the ummms and ahhhs. And when I am finished, she tells me her perspective on the situation. She can hear about what I have seen or interpreted and then, in her straightforward way, give me her take and not in a way that says I read things incorrectly, or misinterpreted the situation. She knows me so well that she knows what I see but also *why* I see things the way I do. Having someone to talk to is one thing, but having someone who really listens to your words and hears what you have to say is something else, something many people do not have. Normally these kinds of chats with Tineka help me calm down because she has seen my crazy and does not judge me. I can open up and share my thoughts with her, and that relieves the stress that would otherwise build up. Anyway, I just wanted to tell Tineka how I felt about this colleague and what he had said; I wanted to get her perspective. It sounds strange, but I was also looking forward to telling her because I thought it would bring us closer as a couple. In my mind the conversation would be a step in the direction of breaking down my lack of understanding of how racial issues manifest in the supposedly diverse, supposedly modern workplace. Tineka would see me open up and then feel more confident, sharing her perspective as well as telling me about her experiences.

We were at home, in our safe space, and I let it all out. I told her the same story I just told you. At points I could hear anger in my own voice.

Then Tineka said, 'Don't act like you are all woke now, Alex. Just because you're married to me doesn't mean you're entitled to get all upset when your Black colleagues say something you think is racially wrong.'

It was a very direct comment, and it somehow hit at everything I was going through internally. His comment was outright unacceptable, and, no matter the circumstance, I would have noticed it and thought about what had happened that day in the office. But if I had not been married to her – a Black woman, am I sure I would have felt so angry? Was I sure that I would have been so shocked? But the fact is I *am* married to

Tineka, and I know she has been treated differently to her White colleagues. I had seen how much that had hurt her. She had also told me about times she had learnt she was getting paid less than her White colleagues, and had to question whether this was due to her level of experience, the fact she is a woman or because she is Black. I have heard her stories and sympathised, but this jolting experience made me begin to question myself and whether I had ever really taken her perspective seriously before.

Her words made me feel uneasy – she was reminding me that, because I am White, I am not entitled to have an opinion on the nuances of racial discrimination between Black people. It made me feel like what I was feeling was fake. Had I been a White man who did not think about racial discrimination and then married a Black woman and started acting differently when I witnessed discrimination? I thought I was someone who had always been sensitive to racism, and made sure I always treated people equally no matter their skin colour. Someone who had always got upset when he saw people acting in a discriminatory or racist way.

TINEKA

Now might be a good time to explain it from my point of view.

It's one thing to try to speak to a White person about discrimination in society, but it is another thing to explain how it exists within the Black community. I know that it is not an excuse, and I should have been more accommodating to Alex when he talked to me about this incident.. Discrimination within the Black community is complex – colourism and self-hate are insidious and ever present. I didn't want to give Alex a history lesson and lecture about Black people living in a world where we are (however subtly) conditioned to think that White is better. We see it in magazines, movies and books. White women are portrayed as prettier, nicer, smarter and more passive. Black women are often portrayed as angry, strong, difficult and not intelligent. And if that has been fed to our society, and in particular the Black community, it isn't a surprise that a Black man would think that Black women are difficult and White people are easier to work with.

So when Alex approached me to complain about his Black workmate preferring to work with White people instead of Black people, I brushed him off, as I assumed that he would not understand the underlying complexities within his colleague's statement – which from my point of view derives from everyday White privilege and superiority. I am not always in the mood to educate or explain race to White people, but after that situation I realised that there was an opportunity to help Alex see things from a different perspective, and me not wanting to explain it caused him to be confused and hurt. Afterwards I did come to understand that I should be more patient when White friends, family or close acquaintances approach me with questions about race. I'm learning to see it more as an opportunity to educate, rather than an opportunity to make them feel bad about themselves.

ALEX

Confession: I want to be more racially aware but I don't need a bogus 'woke badge'.

When I was reeling from Tineka's comment and reflecting on what I have learnt about racism by being married to a Black woman, I focused in on one particular word she had chosen to use.

Woke. That is quite a word, one which needs to be put into context. I do not want to get into a position where I am whitesplaining, so let's quickly look at Urban Dictionary and see what it means. OK, according to Urban Dictionary, 'woke' means 'The act of being very pretentious about how much you care about a social issue'. Now let's check out a different source. The Cambridge Dictionary says 'woke' means 'aware, especially of social problems such as racism and inequality'.

These two explanations may sound quite similar, but there is one word that really stands out for me, and that word is 'pretentious'. So, depending on what you read and trust, being woke might mean you are informed, aware and ready to stand up and educate people about one of the world's most challenging issues, or it may mean you are self-righteous, pompous and politically correct.

Urban Dictionary, unlike the Cambridge Dictionary, is crowdsourced, which means that anyone who is anyone can upload a definition of the word and then other people can vote on how accurate that is. Through this technology Urban Dictionary has become an excellent source for understanding slang words, which often evolve quickly. And because of this I was amazed to see that the top definition I found on Urban Dictionary has over 2,700 votes, yet does not explicitly convey how this word is so rooted in Black culture. What is for sure is that the use of the word 'pretentious' in this definition shows there is a debate between how the word can be used. 'Woke' might sound like a compliment, expressed in a more positive tone such as, 'Oh, he is a pretty woke guy,' but it could also be used to talk badly about someone, for example, 'Ugh, he thinks he is so woke.'

It is also worth considering that woke is a word that is used differently online and offline. Anecdotally, it seems people use the word 'woke' more frequently in tweets and other social media posts rather than in-person conversations in real life, and that has also influenced how its use has evolved and why these definitions are out of sync with the original use of the word. It was first really used by Erykah Badu in 2008. In her song 'Master Teacher' Badu is joined by Bilal and Georgia Anne Muldrow, and they sing about their dream of a more equal world without racial divisions, but they repeatedly remind the audience to 'stay woke'. In this context the expression shows they are not under any illusion about how big the dream they are chasing is. It is a situation that is far from reality, so they repeat 'I stay woke' to show their awareness. This is more or less in sync with what the Cambridge Dictionary seems to tell us. We need to look beyond definitions to grasp just how powerful this word is.

Culture critic Charles Pulliam-Moore has followed the evolution of the expression and explains how 'woke' was once a Black activist watchword closely linked to the #BlackLivesMatter movement. 'Woke' was a word used to show the world you were committed to staying vigilant about social issues. But since then, it has been diluted and taken on a different weight. As Pulliam-Moore writes:

> 'Like "bae," "on fleek," and "bruh," it was only a matter of time before "woke" was co-opted by the mainstream (read: white) internet, but there's a certain tragedy to its loss that's different and more painful.'[9]

It's worth looking at what he means by 'loss' here. What I think he is getting at is that words that once were staples within the Black lexicon have become appropriated, and this takes away their clout when describing characteristics that play an important role in creating and reinforcing Black culture. This suggests White people have corrupted certain words in a way that shows their cultural dominance in society. The words 'bae', 'on fleek' and 'bruh' were used exclusively by Black people at some point to express something unique to Black culture, and it was understood that White people would sound fake by trying to use them. A White person might say 'girlfriend' or 'wife' rather than 'bae', to use his example. But words themselves are not safe from White people, who are not used to losing any aspect of their culture, and when they begin to use these same words, the meaning of those words changes. What someone means by using these words has changed and something has been lost. From his perspective the homogenisation of 'bae' and 'bruh' were a pity, but losing the word 'woke' in this way was tragic because it was once a powerful expression of racial awareness, vigilance and strength.

So when Tineka bluntly told me I was not 'woke', she was using a very specific word – one that has significant history and huge power in a racial context. She was making me check myself, and was talking about a state of mind. She was warning me to avoid false indignation and not lean into Urban Dictionary's definition of the word. Tineka was reminding me that my level of awareness and understanding towards racial issues is limited, and I am locked out of much of this consciousness because of my perspective as a White man.

Yes, I had witnessed one particular racial incident and I had felt the subtle animosity. I had been encouraged by my Black colleague to perpetuate the perspective that Black women are less competent than White men. I had taken two steps forward towards gaining an understanding of discrimination, and I thought my knowledge had advanced. But by discussing my reaction with Tineka I found myself two steps back. I was reminded that I am an outsider in this space and that I shouldn't overreact. I should remember I am little more than a fly on the wall, and this was not a moment that would have an impact on my identity, my people or my life in our society, nor would it be possible for me to have a true understanding of the Black experience.

It would have been a mistake to respond to what I had heard that day by getting on Twitter and publicly shaming my colleague by telling him to #StayWoke. It would have been a mistake because I am a White man and, like lots of different slang words, they take on different meanings when used by different people.

It would be wrong to touch on the word 'woke' in this way and not acknowledge that in October 2019 one of the world's most racially aware leaders actually challenged the entire woke culture. I am talking about the former president of the United States Barack Obama, who said:

> 'I do get a sense sometimes now among certain young people, and this is accelerated by social media, there is this sense sometimes that the way of me making change is to be as judgmental as possible about other people and that's enough. Like if I tweet or hashtag about how you didn't do something right or used the wrong verb, then

I can sit back and feel pretty good about myself because, "Man, did you see how woke I was? I called you out!".'[10]

Later on in that same conversation, Obama said, 'That's not activism. That's not bringing about change. If all you're doing is casting stones, you're probably not going to get that far. That's easy to do.'

I appreciate his straightforward way of addressing this thorny issue. What I think he's saying is that educating people about these complex issues and feelings takes many tricky conversations, trial and error and correction. And by putting himself out there in this way he has pushed a much larger conversation forward, because he challenges people who look up to him to question how they behave and to consider their own actions when it comes to breaking down barriers and creating a dialogue around racism and diversity. It is also worth saying that these exact same words would have felt different and taken on a different meaning if they had been said by another commander in chief or powerful White leader in America. That is what is so crucial to understand here: *who* uses the word 'woke' and their racial profile might actually have an impact on what the word means.

To bring things back to what Tineka said to me: I am not woke just because I am married to a Black woman. Do I want to be woke? Do I want to be pretentious or judgemental? No! Do I want to be aware of social issues and prepared to call someone out if they advance hateful rhetoric? Yes! But will I ever be able to?

At this point I think it would be useful to bring in the words of Katherine Fugate, who has considered these themes. She is well known for writing for the screen, including the TV series *Army Wives*, and feature films *New Year's Eve* and *Valentine's Day*. Here is how she puts it:

> 'No matter how "woke" or evolved I may think I am, I walk this world as a white woman, which means I'll never truly understand what it is to walk this world as a black woman . . . I've had a black male lover. I've had female lovers. I know what discrimination feels like. I've been told I'm going to Hell from family members and from my own religion. Hell, I am a woman . . . That qualifies me, surely? Nope. Still doesn't make me black. No oppression, no misogyny, no religious persecution will ever make me a black woman. I can empathise

but, as someone who is not black in America, I'll never know.'[11]

I have come to think about being woke as part of a spectrum. At one end there is awful bigotry, racism and intolerance. There are well-known hate groups that campaign for racial dominance and political organisations that subvert language and claim to defend 'Christian values', but in essence their message is that anyone who is not White and straight should go to hell. Nobody would ever make the mistake of calling these folk tolerant or woke. And at the other end of the spectrum there are respected individuals who have advanced racial equality in their community and subsequently have been recognised as woke. But there is a wide space in between these two extremes, so it is very possible to be in neither camp. It is not one or the other, woke or racist. And my position on this scale is constantly changing because my perspective shifts as I learn.

At certain moments I have felt like I am moving towards being a racially sensitive person. And these moments feel like progress, as though once the lesson is learnt it remains glued into my thinking and I am not in danger of moving backwards down the spectrum towards being someone who is unaware, blind to racism and intolerance. I make progress and I learn, and then I am in a better position, more comfortable in my own skin and more prepared to be the kind of husband who can play a meaningful role in an interracial marriage.

And then I find myself in situations where all that confidence gets knocked down and I discover, no, I am not as conscious as I thought, and, no, I will never come to a point where I feel that same anger and pain as Tineka. Her indignation and her questions come back to me, such as, 'What has that person been through to behave so badly?' I have been through learnings but there is so much I don't know.

This happened recently, when Tineka and I were in an unexpected altercation with a stranger who disrespected Tineka because of her skin colour. We then disagreed with each other on how best to react to these kinds of ugly racial attacks.

We were walking through a posh part of London. Walking in the other direction on the same pavement were a man and a woman who could have been a couple. The man was Black and the woman was White, and they seemed to be more than friends. When we got close to the other couple, we moved slightly towards the road to make room for them. But the guy suddenly swerved right into Tineka's path and hit his shoulder into hers. There was a moment of collision and her body moved with the impact. Then Tineka turned round and said sharply, 'Excuse *me*.' Then the guy *exploded*, swearing and shouting and escalating things. I could see the woman he was with step back, her mouth open in disbelief. It looked to me that she was just as shocked as I was by this scene, but she was frozen – not making any attempt to calm things down.

I wanted to get us out of the situation before it got any worse, but Tineka stood her ground and fiercely responded to this tall man. 'Wow, really?! What kind of guy are you to think it's OK to push a woman around?!'

I was shocked to see how aggressively the man acted, and I was scared he was going to hit Tineka. At that point I found myself putting my hands up and stepping partially in front of Tineka, putting a physical barrier into the mix. The guy stepped back and looked at me slightly confused, as if he had forgotten I was there. He had been focused on demonstrating to Tineka that he was the dominant force here. It didn't seem like he was at all interested in quarrelling with me, the White guy. I wasn't the target of his aggression.

I was really astounded by how this situation had escalated out of nowhere, and the way Tineka had confronted the stranger with such confidence. So, when Tineka and I had marched off, I told her she needed to be more careful to avoid getting hit. The words came out of my mouth in the form of an instruction: 'Tineka, don't get yourself beaten up.' I was pissed off, and it sounded like I was scolding her or instructing her on how to behave. That is not normally how I talk to Tineka, or adults in general, and Tineka was not pleased.

'I can't believe you are annoyed at *me*,' she said. 'I did nothing wrong. I was just standing there and he completely body-checked me.' And then Tineka said the phrase that I have heard many times before. 'You don't understand because you're White.'

It felt like we were back to that moment when I was telling her about my racist colleague and how I feel when I witness racism. I was yet again confronting this wall between my understanding as a White man and her perspective as a Black woman. It is in these moments I realise just how far away I am from being truly aware of how Tineka is forced to constantly live in fight-or-flight mode because of the way she reads situations and sees the world. The way she feels the need to defend herself and speak up against racial intolerance no matter where it appears.

In order for me to make progress towards being racially aware or woke, how could I boil down these racially charged moments and extract learnings that I can then apply to other situations? Do I just assume *everything* we live through as a couple includes a component that would have been different if we were not an interracial couple or if I was not White? I am constantly searching for answers, for rules and for a method to build my awareness. I want to do this so that I can feel confident in playing a supporting role in our marriage, not because I want other people to think of me as woke. I don't want the badge. Sometimes I make progress; other days it is back to square one, and that is tough.

6

PARENTING IS NOT BLACK OR WHITE

TINEKA

Confession: Spanking traumatised me as a child.

My dad was a fan of the switch – a very thin flexible stick that would be taken off a tree. Picking one was an art – one my dad learnt growing up in the Deep South. A switch had to be thin enough to sting but not leave any marks. Watching my father pick out the switch was often more tortuous than the spanking itself; the anticipation was awful.

My parents, younger sister and I resided in the north-east of the US for a large majority of my life. Despite being nearly 1,000 miles away from his original home of Birmingham, Alabama, my dad made sure he didn't forget his Southern upbringing when it came to disciplining his children. My mom was indifferent, and at times agreed to some extent with my dad about spanking, although they would often argue when she thought he took it a little too far. We lived in the state of South Carolina for a few years, and during that time she worked for the South Carolina Department of Children's Services. Sometimes I could overhear her threatening to report my dad, and it was confusing to me. Because while it wasn't at the intensity or level my dad would spank me, she did it sometimes too.

Both of my parents grew up in the church and, whenever I whined to my mom about why we received spankings when all the other White kids were grounded or punished, she would just say, 'Spare the rod, spoil the child', and start quoting the Bible passage Proverbs xiii, 24, that says, 'Whoever spares the rod hates their children, but the one who loves their children is careful to discipline them.'

While my younger sister would receive spankings every now and then, I received the brunt of it, and, to be fair to my parents, I was no easy child. In fact, I would now consider myself a bit of a nightmare in my early years. My parents also found me annoying, as I could talk for ages and had a comeback for everything. A favourite memory of my father's is from when I was three and broke something very expensive in the house. My sister was a newborn, so she obviously wasn't the culprit. When my dad scolded me about breaking said expensive object, I apparently replied, 'Well, did you see me do it?'

I think part of my knack for trouble was that I was smart. And bored. My parents would later find out through testing that I had a high IQ – in no way a genius but intelligent enough. And I think when smart children have nothing to entertain themselves with, they find entertainment on their own and unfortunately sometimes in not so great ways.

I have to say I have no resentment towards either of my parents for spanking me, even if it did leave me feeling humiliated, traumatised and angry at times. It was how they were disciplined and, I assume, how their parents were disciplined.

If a Black child did anything wrong in the 1960s, they could very well have been killed, and no justice would be served. 'Wrong' could mean unknowingly trespassing on a White person's property, talking back to a White teacher, fighting back if being picked on by a White kid, or simply being too 'smart'. Unfortunately, this is very much still true today, but with the help of social media and, at times, the media, racial injustices are becoming harder to hide.

The fact is this: my parents knew that, as Black children, we couldn't get away with the same things some of the White kids could, and I think they wanted to ensure that I would never do anything that could jeopardise my future. They didn't give me second chances because they knew society wouldn't give me second chances.

I received *a lot* of spankings as a child, and with that constant experience came the uncanny ability to manoeuvre out of spankings at times. One instance was when I picked small gold beads off a headband and decided to see what would happen if I put them into my sister's ear. After the second one she started screaming. We didn't know it at the time, but she had a hole in her ear. I quickly stuck three beads into my own ear, and when my dad came running in, I blamed my sister. My dad was too concerned about her ear to dish out spankings, and we had to spend hours in the clinic, having the beads dug out of our ears. It took around fifteen years for my parents to find out that it was actually me.

Exchanging tips about dealing with spankings with kids my own age became a pastime for me. My greatest piece of advice came from a red-haired freckled White kid who was the son of the youth pastor at my church. It was then I learnt Black parents are not the only ones who spank their kids – although I've met very few

White kids with parents who did. We were complaining about having sore bottoms, as we both had received spankings the day before. Like me, he also had a knack for getting in trouble.

'I usually don't even care about getting spankings any more,' he said.

'Why wouldn't you care? It hurts!' I responded.

'Well, because I usually put on, like, a bunch of underwear and then I don't even cry; I don't even feel anything. I didn't have time to do it before I got spanked yesterday, though.'

'Ah, wow, that is such a cool idea!' I exclaimed. 'I'm gonna try that next time.'

And so when my next spanking rolled around, I felt nothing. Just the pressure of my dad's hand as it hit my bottom. And after some time, my dad said, 'Wait a minute, how come you're not crying or anything?'

'Huh?' I said, looking up innocently into my dad's eyes. 'I don't know,' I said nervously.

Then my dad began to poke my bottom and said, 'Hold on, this feels very soft . . . What the . . . ' And then he peeked at the ten pairs of underwear I was wearing and started laughing hysterically.

He laughed for a good ten minutes, struggling to catch his breath.

'You are kooky, do you know that?' he said. Then he gave me a big hug and walked out of the room, chuckling to himself. And that was how I escaped many spankings – simply humouring my dad. If I could get him to laugh, I was home free. Although, of course, the times I would actually try never worked, and the times I didn't try, did.

There was one day I was feeling extra dramatic. And when my dad went to hit my bottom I started screaming before anything actually happened.

'I haven't even hit you yet!' my dad exclaimed, clearly amused.

After the fourth time of this happening, he said, laughing, 'You are something else,' and walked out of the room.

My dad used to always say, 'Don't let your mouth write a cheque that your butt can't cash.' That expression often means 'talk is cheap', but my dad used it in a very different way. His meaning was simply that if I said something disrespectful, I'd get a spanking. Plain and simple. So, when going out, I would negotiate with him about exactly how he wanted me to behave so that I could *avoid* a spanking. This is exactly what he wanted me to learn: that I can and should adjust my behaviour according to the expectations of people and society. I should behave the way others want me to – not the way I want to. Thinking back, I know my dad came from a time when, in order to survive, you needed to act according to society's standards. But real change never happened by people doing what others wanted them to.

And, as time went on, that became the cycle of my life at home: avoiding spankings. Family and friends would comment, 'Wow, she's so well behaved; she's stayed in her seat for hours not making a peep.'

As soon as those phrases were uttered, I'd sigh in relief, knowing I had been good enough to escape a sore bottom for the evening. I would refuse to play with other kids. I would refuse to watch television, and I wouldn't talk. Not talking was very important because 'children were meant to be seen and not heard', as my dad would often say. Although getting spanked didn't stop me from being so-called 'naughty'. All the crying, pain and humiliation didn't stop me from being my childish self. I think if my parents had known it wouldn't have an immediate effect on my behaviour, perhaps they could have found a different avenue or method for disciplining. It certainly would have saved a lot of heartache. And it does make me think that perhaps spanking any children Alex and

I might decide to have would not be such a good thing. Perhaps spanking should depend on the child, parents and situation, and not just be a be-all and end-all. I know my parents did their best to raise me to thrive in a society that was not built for someone like me. But spanking never really stopped me from misbehaving. Knowing the trauma I've experienced from spanking and the humiliation I felt, while it may work for some parents, I do not want to inflict the same discipline on someone else. But I also know that we never truly know how we'll act or behave in situations until they happen – and that's something I want to acknowledge. Maybe one day I will come to see and understand the thinking behind my parents' form of discipline, or perhaps I never will.

When my parents spanked me, it was never really about them or me. It was about how society treats me. They spanked me in order to adjust my behaviour so that society (White people) accepted me to exist around them. But I don't want to have to encourage any potential children to adapt to society's norms for their own safety and success. I don't know what the world will be like in the future; perhaps we'll live somewhere like Scotland, where spanking is illegal, and this won't even be a consideration. In the meantime, I can only focus on projects such as this book and Huetribe, to contribute my small part in changing society for the better and creating a world I would actually want any non-White children I might have to live in.

While all may not agree, in my experience, spanking is not uncommon in the Black community. And I have many Black friends and family members who consider spanking or using the switch to be normal. In fact, they are thankful for the way their parents disciplined them – it taught them how to discipline themselves and survive in a world that can be unforgiving if you're not White. Sometimes it's what many of us feel we are doing in this insidious racial climate – just trying to survive. I know that the person I am today is only because of my parents. However, there were some instances that traumatised me as a child and that I still become emotional about as an adult today. One of those instances is a moment that started with an act of kindness. And, as they say, no good deed goes unpunished.

Around the age of seven, I started attending an after-school youth centre. The centre had numerous activities, and we'd hang out for about three to four hours until our parents picked us up. Over time, like most kids, I made friends. And I've always been a loyal friend, even as a child. I like to think of friends as the family we choose for ourselves, and so I have always had a soft spot for friends in need. During the summer, the youth centre was open all day, and this is where I spent most of my time during the humid and hot South Carolina days. While hanging out at a table playing checkers with a few friends, one of my friends cried out, 'Oh no, where are my glasses?'

'Where did you last see them?' I asked.

'Right here on the table!'

And she was freaking out. I mean, a scared-for-her-life type of reaction.

And then she said a sentence that would create a horrific experience for me down the line.

'My parents are going to kill me,' she said through tears. She stood there sobbing frantically, looking under the game boards in hope.

Wow, I thought. Her parents are actually going to *kill* her. Over a pair of *glasses*. I felt for her, I really did. And, as the end of the day approached, she grew more and more upset. So, finally, I went up to a counsellor and I said, 'I accidently threw her glasses in the trash can.'

'Thank you for telling us that,' the counsellor said.

Now, you have to understand that I was more naive than most kids my age. In fact, my friends often made fun of me for my lack of 'worldliness'. And even my younger sister was often surprised and annoyed at my lack of social understanding, which many kids my age already had.

My dad would often pick me up from the centre after school. And when he did on this occasion, the counsellor said nothing. And I didn't even think anything of the incident. In my childish mind I thought nothing would come of it. I had just saved my friend from getting killed by her parents. She was relieved when I had said it, unaware that I had actually lied for her. It was a good day for all.

The next day, around lunchtime, while playing ping-pong in the main hall with a few friends, my dad appeared. I saw him in his handsome white naval uniform, complete with his sailor's hat and polished black shoes. I thought it was odd to see him at that time of day but, nevertheless, I waved to him in excitement. He didn't wave back, and he didn't smile. I ran over to him to give him a hug and, as I did, he pulled me away from him.

He silently pulled up a nearby chair, calmly slipped the back of my trousers below my bottom and gently placed me over his knee. Before I knew what was happening, he was spanking me in front of around thirty children aged seven to eleven.

The counsellor had waited until that morning to call him. She had told him that I had thrown my friend's glasses out, causing her much distress. You have to understand, a talkative smart Black girl living in the Deep South in the early 1990s annoyed some of the White counsellors. In fact, I had one who purposely made fun of names she considered *too* Black. That particular counsellor enjoyed calling me *Tin-ee-goo* instead of *Tin-ee-ka.* She could tell it made me uncomfortable, but I didn't know what to say. And any chance to tell my parents I had done something wrong (or any of the other minority children for that matter), they took. I knew their treatment of me at the time was off, but as a child I couldn't place it, and my parents hadn't really started talking to me about the gravity of race at that age. But, looking back, those were some of my first encounters with racial microaggressions.

With my rear end exposed, being slapped intensely in a pattern-like drumbeat, I started wailing. I kicked and pleaded, with tears streaming down my face.

'I didn't do it, Daddy!' I yelled over and over.

But he continued to spank me, his face emotionless.

This spanking hurt more than others, partly because my dad was furious, and partly because of the humiliation.

All the kids gathered round in a semicircle to watch – most of them White. No one laughed, no one pointed. They were confused, scared and somewhat curious, I believe, their blank faces displaying an array of emotions.

I was so confused. My dad had always said we had to behave so we didn't look crazy in front of White people. And now he was humiliating me in front of all of them.

I continued screaming, and my dad uttered phrases in between each slap to my bottom.

'Are you going to do that again, huh?!'

'No, Daddy, I promise. I didn't even do it!'

He thought I was lying when I said I didn't do it, and felt he wasn't getting through to me, so he hit my bottom harder.

'We *SLAP* don't *SLAP* touch *SLAP* other *SLAP* people's *SLAP* things!' *SLAP*

After about fifteen minutes of me crying, begging and screaming, I could feel my dad's arm getting tired. The counsellors finally started to feel uncomfortable (they had been watching the entire time too), and escorted the rest of the kids out of the main recreational hall and into another room.

My father eventually stopped, his face still without emotion. He quietly picked up the chair put it back and walked away. I pulled up the back of my pants, wiped my eyes and watched him walk away. I then went to join the other kids and started playing board games silently.

No one said a word. I think they all felt sorry for me. Not the counsellors, though. They glanced over at me as I walked out of the main hall – their faces a reflection of hidden intentions.

My dad had to buy the girl in question new glasses and apologise to her parents, who thought I was a 'troubled' kid. But I wasn't. It was simply that a White counsellor didn't believe me when I said it was an accident. Would she have believed a White child? Most likely. But this woman's one decision created a traumatic moment for me that would last a lifetime.

Yet one of the most profound lessons I ever learnt from my dad was through the very act of him *not* spanking me. We had moved to a town on the coast of South Carolina, to a great neighbourhood. The nearest school, however, was labelled one of the worst schools in the state. It had a history of violence and drunken principals, and the children – my fellow classmates – lived in horrific conditions. I was grateful the school bus always dropped the kids living in impoverished neighbourhoods off first on the way home, so they wouldn't see my house or the neighbourhood I lived in. I was already an outsider – they called me 'White girl' because of the way I talked, made fun of the way I dressed and asked if I had a weave in my hair before I knew what a weave was. They never picked on the White kids, though. On one particular day the bus driver took an alternate route and I was dropped off first. We stopped at my house and I ran off the bus as quickly as I could – the only Black kid in a line of White kids stepping off the bus. I didn't know at the time why I felt bad or ashamed, but I remember thinking surely it didn't seem right that more Black kids didn't live in the same neighborhood as me.

In order to fit in I tried to be tougher, talk differently and started getting into fights to be 'cool'. After I would get into a fight, other students in my class would say to me, 'You did OK. You didn't win it, but you did OK.' I had some children in my class who were also clearly being abused by their parents. They would come in with a black eye and give an excuse that didn't make sense. I never understood why the teachers – all of them White – didn't ask questions or say anything. I realise now they simply didn't care. Those kids picked on me the most, but I never fought back; I understood why they were always angry.

In the middle of the school year a new girl joined our class. She was nice, calm and very smart; she was also White. We became friends quickly and got along for some time. But one day we argued over a grade I received. You see, the teacher in our class would often leave the room for hours at a time, and also allowed the kids to grade each other's tests – and never checked them. So if you had a friend grade your test, you could end up being a straight-A student and not know a thing. But if you ended up with a frenemy grading your test, you could end up failing while you might actually be the smartest kid in the class. My friend, she was just being honest. She had given me a failing mark. Honestly, as our teacher wasn't actually teaching us anything, it's no surprise I failed. I was upset because others had given me failing marks before when the answers were right. I assumed she was just doing it out of spite. We lived a few doors down from each other, so after we stepped off the bus one day and walked past her house, I pushed her and yelled, 'You better watch your back. I'm going to get you later!' She was clearly scared, and quietly ran into her house. I walked down the street proud of myself for showing her that I meant business.

My dad arrived in the early evening, and a few minutes later we heard the doorbell ring. 'Who could that be?' my dad asked – eyeing me suspiciously. I guess he had already sensed it had something to do with me.

Well, it turns out my friend's mom had overheard what I yelled at her. And her dad just so happened to know my father. I listened behind the wall as I overheard my friend's dad telling the story and he repeated to my dad what I had said. When the door closed, my dad screamed at me in a way he never had before.

'You're a bully now?!' he said, shaking his head in disbelief. 'I bet you didn't know that her mom was home and I actually work with her dad! I try my best to teach you how to be a good person and this is what happens – unbelievable.' To top it off, my report card came back the next day – all Cs. I didn't receive a spanking but I waited for it, wearing several pairs of underwear all day, just in case he jumped from behind a corner and surprised me. Weeks passed, and nothing. My dad avoided talking to me, walking around the house silent and solemn. He refused to sign my report card, something he loved doing. My grades always made him proud. I'd get a ninety-two on a test, and he would say, 'Very nice job, sweetheart, but next time try to get a hundred, OK?'

My fifth-grade graduation was coming up and I was preparing a surprise for my parents – my dad in particular. I had been practising for months as the soloist to open our graduation with a chorus of thirty younger students. I was singing a song about Kwanzaa, an African-American celebration of life that takes place over the Christmas holiday period. I was even given an African-print dress to wear. I wanted to show my dad that I at least had some awareness of my roots and I knew he would love it. But he was still so angry about me bullying another girl, especially a White one. He refused to go. But I still went and performed in front of hundreds of people. Yet all I could do was look out in the audience and not see the one person I wanted to see me perform. After that, I went home. I never mentioned the performance, and I'm not sure my mom said anything about it to him either – reminding him he missed my show may have just made things worse. As I got into bed that night, I cried myself to sleep. I would rather have had the spanking. From that day on I tried to make sure I didn't bully anyone ever again. My dad's disgust with what I had done and the fact he didn't even want to be near me had taught me enough. I never wanted him or anyone else to look at me that way again. I don't think my dad even realised the life-long lesson he taught me, and he did it without having to lift a finger. So while spanking does have value, it really can have unforeseen negative repercussions that result in emotional and sometimes psychological issues for children. And for many years as a child I feared him as much as I loved him. There are more ways than one to prepare someone for the ways of the world, more ways than one to have an impact and teach a lesson.

ALEX

Confession: I know that if I have mixed-race children, they won't have my privilege – and I don't know what to do about it.

My comfortable upbringing has moulded my thinking around what I want for my kids when, hopefully, my wife and I form a family. I want them to feel loved. Like all parents, I badly want to provide for them in both the material and the emotional sense. But will I be ready? Will I be able? How could I be equipped to handle their inevitable questions of identity as mixed-race people?

Talking this through with my wife in the hypothetical sense is one step. But dealing with it face to face will be a totally different matter. Our half-Black, half-White children will navigate the world differently, and I worry about what happens when I need to provide answers to questions I myself have never had to ask.

On an episode of her podcast, *Pretty Big Deal,* model Ashley Graham spoke about this issue. The thirty-three-year-old, who has been married for many years to a Black man, spreads an important message for White people in interracial relationships. Here is how she phrases it:

> 'Being a White woman, who will potentially have children who will be Black, I have to switch my mind. I have to completely say, "Wow. I was never raised like that . . ." All the White women out there or all the White guys out there, you have to have these conversations when you're in these relationships because, as a White person, we live in a White world.'[12]

By reminding some listeners that they live in a 'White world' Graham makes the point that a White person can operate within a very different reality and frame of reference to the Black person they are sharing their life with. And just by acknowledging how different these realities are, couples can find a space to discuss their own individual issues and properly make sense to their partner. She is not saying the two realities are incompatible or somehow in conflict with one another, just that it is important to acknowledge this difference and move forward with a better understanding of where your partner is coming from, and that can only be done through conversation.

While all children have different life experiences, it is clear to me that many mixed-race children have a path plotted for them, a path that is not as smooth and open as the one that little White kids walk on. They will ask: where do I fit in this world? Why are my friends different from me? Why don't I see role models I can relate to and learn from? Why are there so few people in power who look like me? As a White man I can engage with these questions on an academic level, but I cannot *live* them. I can't feel the layers of confusion or the depth of bewilderment my children will have to carry.

After I read *Between the World and Me* by Ta-Nehisi Coates, my thinking on this topic evolved. The touching narrative is in the form of an intimate letter to the author's teenage son.

> 'I write you in your 15th year . . . And you know now, if you did not before, that the police departments of your country have been endowed with the authority to destroy your body. I tell you now that the question of how one should live within a Black body, within a country lost in the Dream,

is the question of my life, and the pursuit of this question, I have found, ultimately answers itself.'[13]

Coates gives a powerful insight into the way a Black father might pass down advice to his Black son. He has chosen to do this in a way that is shocking, because what he describes could be so frightening to a teenager. But at the same time his status as a Black man gives him a position of authority in this dynamic, and that is why the lesson will stick in the son's mind. The father shows the son that 'the question of how one should live within a Black body' is not simply existence, but a question, a conundrum. This is a warning that other people, White people with authority, will stand in the way of existence, inflict violence upon your people and leave the Black son unsure about his legitimacy and his right to happiness and fulfilment.

As well as Coates, I also wanted to read about the specific struggle mixed-race families and children encounter. I stumbled upon some words that really struck me in a blog post Kassidy Mi'chal wrote for the Creative Mental Health Awareness Initiative in 2017.

'Many mixed-race children have to deal with serious identity issues that can follow them well into adulthood, the constant battle between seeking refuge

> within a racial group while still maintaining a true sense of self is perilous. These kids evolve into adulthood with virtually no clue surrounding their unique culture. They may take on the charisma or traits of their dominant race, but there is always something there that sets them apart.'[14]

That comfortable feeling of being surrounded by people who understand you, and know what you are going through, is so important in growing confidence and developing who you are. And what Mi'chal is saying here is that, without that experience of commonality, people can feel lost or torn when it comes to being comfortable in their own skin. So because of this yearning to belong, some mixed-race children may extenuate certain aspects of who they are and hide other traits.

This description of the identity struggle that mixed-race children go through made a lot of sense to me, but after reading it I did not have a real picture in my mind about what this struggle would look like in the real world.

Then I saw a tweet about children trying to understand and confront racism. A short message jumped out from my feed and smacked me in the face. The tweet from the exceptional BBC news anchor Lukwesa Burak read: *About to go on air after a tearful conversation with my daughter who asked why a boy at school told her she should be in the black bin because her skin is dirty. THIRD incident.*[15]

Lukwesa spent her early years living in Zambia, before moving to the UK when she was eight years old. I guess she had some personal experience to draw on when responding to her daughter's pain. I guess she was able to properly empathise through her own understanding formed by her experience. The very fact Lukwesa sent this tweet out into the world suggests an ability to face this very real, very painful situation head-on. I doubt I could do the same if I had to deal with that kind of conflict right now.

But then I thought about a good friend of mine who is White, and is actually working through this issue, and is thinking every day about how he can help his young son grow into a person who is proud of his identity as a person with diverse heritage.

My friend is a White British man and, like me, also in his early thirties. His wife was born in the Caribbean, emigrated to the USA and is now a US citizen. Their adorable son is mixed-race, and I first met him when he was just three months old. Clearly at that age he was totally unaware of his racial identity and how it will inevitably have some kind of impact on the way he experiences the world and how certain people respond to him. But nonetheless his parents were already faced with those challenges.

My friend explained that if you search for 'nursery rhymes' on YouTube, you are presented with millions of results within seconds. Gone are the days of going to the bookshelf and picking out a book with a battered front cover, faded illustrations and pages stained with drool and bits of food. On YouTube there are videos of animated stars singing 'Twinkle Twinkle', purple cats singing 'The Wheels on the Bus Go Round and Round'. There are videos of cartoon mice, who look like monsters, singing 'Hickory Dickory Dock'. There are songs in English, French, Spanish, Japanese, Swahili and a whole host of other languages.

'I have to choose,' my friend explained. 'Will we have the traditional White Western songs sung by White cartoons before bed, or do I select the Black African songs where the characters are from Nigeria, Kenya or South Africa if I can't find videos of mixed-race cartoon characters singing the songs my parents sung me when I was a child. I want my son to see characters that look like him, singing songs from both of his cultures. I want him to feel from the very start of his life that he is a unique person but also part of a group of people who are like him – neither White nor Black.'

This was an incredibly eye-opening conversation. I know that mixed-race children are left out of so many conversations, so why would I expect the community of content creators who are actively uploading to YouTube to be different? How is it that there is a lack of nursery rhymes showing mixed-race children singing and discovering the world? It frustrates me a great deal that this area of learning is grappling with the world in a new way, a cycle of hoping for greater acceptance followed by learning that, no, this reality permeates every single part of our lives, even in the digital age, where Google learns about us in order to suggest products we would want. It reminded me of why Tineka and I felt the need to create Huetribe, and I felt proud we were doing something positive to impact the marketplace, which is not set up for people like this child.

I admire my friends for being so thoughtful and caring, and really taking the time to search through so many different songs while considering the challenge through a racial lens. Caring for their child's development as any parent would, but not underestimating the reality that their child is going to be challenged in ways other children will not be. Challenged in ways they were not when they were growing up. They could so easily select the 'Best Songs for Kids' YouTube playlist and join the millions of subscribers, but they realise this easy way out is not enough for their son in his mixed-race context.

7

DISCRIMINATION KNOWS NO BORDERS

ALEX

Confession: It sucks that judging eyes follow us even when we travel.

I caught the travel bug young. A very early memory I have is being on a plane that is still on the runway. In the memory everything is loud and screechy. My dad is in the seat next to me. He taps me on the shoulder and shows me I should put my hands over my ears. He is talking while he does the hand motions, but in the memory I just see his mouth forming the words. Then in the memory the volume gets turned down and it ends.

I know now that I was travelling on a family holiday to Portugal. At the time I was probably four years old, and I had no concept of what it meant to go from one country to another. I just knew it was a big deal that we were doing this 'flying' thing, and I was very, very excited.

Since then I have been fortunate to travel a lot – with my family, by myself, with friends and with my wife. I have had all kinds of experiences on the road in Africa, America, Asia, Australia and Europe, which have given me food for thought. *Why* do I do this? What is the point of leaving the comfort of your own home to move around the world? By stepping out of your comfort zone and exposing yourself to the outside world you don't know who you might meet and what kinds of danger you might find. And when I have travelled with Tineka, we have found ourselves having challenging and heated debates as we have tried to escape unwanted attention and understand why interracial couples are perceived and treated differently in certain parts of the world.

Maybe the most exhilarating aspect about taking a trip is you get a break from your normal life. When we travel to new countries, Tineka and I always look for opportunities to reinvigorate ourselves, shake up our assumptions and breathe some fresh air. We both enjoy seeking out new food – I love it when I shock my taste buds – and when I wake myself up and remember that my day-to-day reality is just one reality. My 'normal life' is actually not normal at all. I am even reminded that, in certain more conservative cultures, people are not exposed to the possibility of living their life with someone who is racially different from them. When

I travel, I get to see how my life and understanding of the world would be very different if I was born into a different family or in a different context.

Pico Iyer's essays and books on what it means to live life in search of adventure have inspired me and given me lots of food for thought. In an essay he wrote in March 2000, he puts it like this:

> 'We travel, then, in part just to shake up our complacencies by seeing all the moral and political urgencies, the life-and-death dilemmas, that we seldom have to face at home . . . Travel is the best way we have of rescuing the humanity of places, and saving them from abstraction and ideology.'[16]

When I first read those words some fifteen years ago, I thought the message was that people who have the means to travel benefit from gawking at life-and-death dilemmas or shocking scenes of poverty. Tourists get to feel better about their lot because they can put their life into perspective after seeing the way others are forced to live. They can breathe a sigh of relief and tell themselves, 'Well, at least I don't have to live like *that*.'

But since then I have grown and had some harsh experiences that have changed my thinking, especially about what Iyer means when he talks of saving places from abstraction and ideology.

What I think Iyer means is we often have one fairly general, abstract idea of what a place is like – an idea that has been formed in our minds through the media and the stories we hear from friends and relatives who have been there – but this is rarely accurate. Tineka had told me loads about what Alabama is like, and I had seen the film *Forrest Gump* before I actually travelled there with her, for instance. I had heard the stories and seen some of her photos, and through those influences I had constructed in my mind a crude concept of what it would be like: farmland and sweet tea, people with strange accents who prefer to take life at a gentle pace. But when I went myself, met people from there and saw how they got on with daily life, and how they treated Tineka and me, my abstract ideas were shattered as I got a much more immersive experience. I never thought people would be so warm and welcoming to an outsider like me, and I never considered that pancake parlours would serve maple syrup warm. My experiences in restaurants were also surprising, but not because of the food. I didn't see any table except ours, where White people and Black people were sitting and eating together. I was also surprised that I was the one who noticed that dynamic, rather than Tineka.

When you visit a new destination, there is a limit on how much preparation you can do in advance, because you will see things in a certain way at a certain moment in the life of that place, and that means you have an experience of a place that is true for you. When you see a place with fresh eyes, you are in a particular moment of your life, which means you have certain concerns and an experience that makes sense to you. This all means you save town and cities from this abstraction.

For Tineka and me a big difference when it comes to the travel experience happens even before we head to the airport or train station. Tineka often gets nervous before travelling because in some cultures it is unusual to see Black women. Tineka often anticipates being treated with curiosity or a lack of respect, especially when it comes to her personal space. It can be nerve-racking for Tineka to think about what people we meet in foreign countries will assume when they see a Black woman travelling with a White man. In some cases there are subtle gestures or exchanges in hotels that reveal how people can be surprised to see a person of colour with money, and that impacts Tineka's experience while travelling.

Practically, this means Tineka spends far more time researching a destination than I do. I will find her reading about women's rights and crime rates in countries we travel to, as well as the ethnic composition of society and the cultural history. Before we go on a trip, I will probably be looking at photos of beaches and hotels, but Tineka will be scouring the internet, seeking out blogs on what other people from minority groups have experienced when they have travelled there. One written piece Tineka showed me was an article in *The Boston Globe* called 'Black, American, and abroad? Racism travels free'. The author, Jeneé Osterheldt, describes being attacked by a White woman while trying to catch a cab in Paris and concludes: 'There is no escaping racism. It comes with you in the carry-on bag called your skin.'[17] It is shocking to read about such incidents and learn about how intolerant people can be. I agree we should read about this reality in a foreign place, but a part of me wishes these articles would have less of an impact on Tineka and not make her feel so apprehensive about travelling. When I read this piece by Osterheldt, I began thinking about how absurd it is that our skin colour even influences the kind of travel advice we digest. I have been to places where all travellers need to exercise caution, but I have never travelled to a destination where I was advised to behave in a certain way because of my white skin. Perhaps this lack of specific advice has influenced me and allowed me to develop such a nonchalant attitude when packing a bag and roaming around a foreign country. It is a clear double standard that Tineka and I experience, discuss and criticise, but I want Tineka to feel safe and know she is travelling with someone who will keep her safe. But I have learnt that, no matter what I want, it is impossible to ignore or gloss over an entire attitude culture when it is so uniformly White and shocked by the sight of an interracial couple.

Sure, we like to travel to get a break from our daily lives, but there are some difficult realities that persist, no matter where we go in the world. Tineka and I have travelled together to countries like Croatia, India, the USA, Italy, the Netherlands, Nepal and Thailand, and in all these locations we have felt a lot of attention – people staring at us, behaving in a way that makes us think they are questioning us as a couple. There have been mocking laughs, grabbing and people taking photos without asking.

To give a recent example, we went to Croatia to get away, relax and enjoy the Adriatic Sea. This was just a few years ago, in 2012, and Tineka had told a few friends how excited she was about the trip. One of her Black male friends at the time responded with a warning: people in the Western Balkans aren't really used to seeing Black people, and Tineka's experience bore that out.

During our trip, Tineka was stared at, stalked and followed around by people with cameras. Some people literally leapt out of the way when they saw us coming; others asked to take a photo with us for the family album! It was as if they wanted a memento so they could tell their grandkids about that time they saw a real-life Black woman on the beach. Tineka told me she felt like an alien, and I was left trying to comfort her and find distractions. But in reality I had no idea how to avoid the gawping and process this onslaught of unwanted attention. It was so exhausting being stared at so much that by the end of the day we avoided bars and missed out on experiencing the famous nightlife. We were worried that the cocktail of alcohol and ignorant curiosity could spell danger for us.

Luckily, we had booked a boat cruise, and there was a mixture of nationalities on board: Americans,

Norwegians, Swedes, Germans and Italians. Most of us became fast friends and stuck together each time we docked and went exploring on land.

During one of these excursions, a baby spotted us when we walked past a café and the baby broke into tears! The crying prompted the parents to put down their drinks and try to understand what was wrong with the child. Did he need his nappy changing? Was he hungry? They looked around and then out in the same direction the baby was looking. After some time, they realised that the baby was crying because he had spotted a Black person, and the confusion was overwhelming.

The parents burst out laughing and explained what was happening to their friends. They saw how ridiculous it was that the baby was reacting in this way, but they didn't need to make a scene and point at Tineka and make her feel like a comedic object. It was how the adults reacted that annoyed me the most, because it felt insensitive – a child doesn't know how to act, but the parents should have known better. They didn't spend a second considering how Tineka would feel, seeing tears roll down a baby's face, and actually made things worse for us by enjoying the moment. Tineka put her head down as we moved away from the café, clearly hurt by having to deal with something that her White travel companions did not. Tineka even started positioning herself in the middle of our group of White tourists when walking, so fewer people would see her. She proceeded to make herself smaller or nearly invisible. I wanted her to be her normal self, full of life and expressive, but her behaviour showed me just how much she felt the stares and how hard that was for her.

Confession: Stereotyping makes me mad. Avoid these mental shortcuts; they can have a seriously negative impact.

When Tineka and I have travelled outside Europe, we have also experienced people treating us differently and making assumptions about us, which we found strange, judgemental and just plain unnecessary. Well-travelled friends warned us that interracial couples can be an unusual sight in parts of Thailand, and while it has long been a destination for tourists of all nationalities, some people there are still wary or untrusting of foreigners.

Tineka, myself and my sister travelled to a coastal area in Thailand called Ao Nang. There were sandy beaches with palm trees and a beautiful stretch of ocean perfect for swimming. We decided to stay in a simple hotel with just a few rooms. The three of us went to the reception area to check in. The receptionist began welcoming us, telling us about the local beaches and restaurants – the entire time trying (rather unsuccessfully) to hide her confusion as to our group dynamic. Her expression said it all: how did a White man, a White woman and a Black woman know each other? We had booked one double room and one single room for our stay. The receptionist could have simply placed the keys down on the counter for us to pick up, but, no, she passed them to us in a way that showed her assumption: the two White people must be the couple and this Black person is their friend tagging along.

When the right keys eventually found themselves in the right hands, we exchanged awkward glances, but the receptionist had a nice smile on her face. She had worked out who was who.

After a few days enjoying the local beaches, we took a boat tour to see some of the natural beauty. There were ten to fifteen people on board and we drifted off slowly into the bay. When we reached the open ocean, the skipper cranked up the motors, and cranked up the sound system. One of the crew started chatting to my sister, who explained that she was from England and that she was travelling with her brother and his girlfriend. Simple, friendly chit-chat.

When she introduced this crew member to Tineka, his eyes lit up and he went for a fist bump. Tineka slowly and awkwardly fist bumped this man and said hello, but clearly did not expect what was to come next. This Thai tour operator, who was wearing a faded Red Bull shirt and plastic flip-flops, rolled up his sleeves to show off tattoos of famous rappers. 'Yeah, Biggie Smalls, Tupac, Dr. Dre. I love all that shit,' he said with his Thai accent. 'Which rappers do you love?' Then he threw up his deuces and started rapping to Tineka, 'Compton, East Side, West Side . . . Living in a gangsta's paradise.'

Tineka's face glazed over. The look she has when she's trying to control herself from getting cross.

'I don't listen to that much rap actually,' she said. 'African-Americans are also into other types of music.'

But he didn't hear a word – he just kept loudly talking about gangstas and rap.

Was this man trying to make Tineka feel like she had found a 'homie', as he put it, despite being so far from home?

We were stuck on a boat with this dude. Tineka couldn't escape his cultural appropriation, and none of us wanted to risk offending him in case he flipped out and decided to throw us overboard. We realised some of the other passengers were observing the scene with some amusement. Why wouldn't they? We were literally their entertainment. I found myself wondering what to say. Do I insist he stop embarrassing himself and making Tineka feel awkward? Should I just sit back and enjoy the weird karaoke? Was it worth starting a discussion on the topic of the varieties of Black culture in the US? I realise now I should have taken the chance to quietly educate this man about his behaviour and explain why he should just stop, but before I got a chance to choose my tactic, we hit some waves and the captain had to focus all his energies on steering us to safety in a nearby cove. This well-timed distraction gave us a moment to move to a different part of the boat, enjoy the scenery and collect ourselves.

Clearly the man's behaviour was racially motivated. When he found out I was from the UK, he didn't burst out into song and start singing The Beatles. He hadn't put me in a box in the same way he had done with Tineka.

Tineka later told me how the interaction took her by surprise. She didn't let it get under her skin, but she was annoyed.

'It's not even an original stereotype,' Tineka told me. I could see she was trying to move past this unfortunate incident, where a man who probably doesn't get much chance to interact with Black people had taken one look at Tineka, picked out one of her physical features and then proceeded to tell her who she was. And this is how stereotyping actually works in tandem with prejudice to maintain or highlight inequalities in our society. By seeing Tineka's black skin he didn't make an attempt to get to know who Tineka was as an individual, or what kind of music she liked. No, he just lumped her in with this idea he had of what all Black people are like.

This encounter has stuck with me. In fact, Tineka and I have spoken about it many times since, both alone and with close friends. I think it stuck in my mind because music connects us as a couple. We both have an eclectic appreciation of music, but hearing what Tineka is listening to, what sounds and lyrics are inspiring her, helps me see another side of who she is.

Tineka and I were both exposed to all kinds of music from a young age. She has told me many times about the fond memories she has of going on road trips with her dad in the US, when he would turn up the radio when Sam Cooke's song 'Chain Gang' came on.

For me the earliest memory I have connected to music came courtesy of Tracy Chapman. As young kids, my older brother and I would be sitting in the back seat of the car and my dad would put on the song 'Fast Car'. I am sure that being exposed to music with strong messages so early on shaped me and influenced the sorts of messages I want to hear in music.

Whenever my mum drove, she would play Celine Dion, but I think that was just because we asked her to, rather than because she actually loved the music. Her passion was playing classical music on the piano at home, practising over and over again until she was note-perfect.

And ever since meeting Tineka I have enjoyed her passion for music and her extremely eclectic taste. One of the first memories I have of really feeling close to her is the day she introduced me to Bruce Springsteen's song 'Blinded by the Light', which was covered by Manfred Mann's Earth Band. We were at a house party with a group of friends, talking about songs we liked, when Tineka asked me whether I'd ever heard it. When I said no, we stepped out of the party, she took out her big clunky iPod and earphones and we sat on the cold concrete listening to this rock anthem, which blew me away.

I wanted this boat captain in Thailand to see all these layers and look at himself in the mirror. He didn't look anything like Jay-Z or Tupac or Nas, but he was a huge fan of their music. That's cool. Just because Tineka has the same skin colour as these guys, and they come from the same country, doesn't mean she is necessarily a fan of their music.

Another place that was challenging for us to visit was Romania. On this occasion Tineka was not the only one researching the places we were going to visit, because I had no idea what we might encounter there, or what Romanian people were like. It was not as if we were going for a weekend city break.

We were invited to travel to a small town in the countryside outside the capital city which is the hometown of two close friends who are both men. We went to take part in a food festival, which usually attracts over 2,000 people.

I was excited to be invited, but Tineka was nervous. Her skin colour had attracted unwanted attention during a previous trip in Eastern Europe, so we were glad to have local guides with us who would help us discover the nicest features of the town and steer us clear of any danger.

From the start of our trip to Romania Tineka made it clear she didn't feel comfortable. At the beginning of the trip we went to a café with our two friends and one of them also invited their mum. At one point Tineka told me some men were pointing and laughing at her. I told her to ignore them but got a quick response.

'It's easy for you to say. It's not happening to you.'

And it took me some time to accept this was true. In fact, most people saw my white skin and only realised I wasn't Romanian when I spoke.

When we paid our bill and went to exit the café, a woman and her young child were ordering pastries from the counter. They were chatting away in Romanian and our friends said something in Romanian to the mum and daughter. Smiling, they turned back to us and explained that the child had asked her mother to look at Tineka and had then said, 'Why is her skin that colour?' The mum had paused and told her, 'Yes, she's very beautiful.' Apparently the child kept saying, 'No, why is her skin *that* colour?'

Our friends had told the child that Tineka had eaten too much chocolate when she was young and that was why she had dark skin.

The child paused and nodded with a sort of understanding.

Tineka was upset that they had missed the opportunity to start a proper conversation about what it means to be White and what it means to be Black and how important it is to treat all people the same, irrespective of their skin tone, height or weight.

I agreed that our friends had taken the situation into their own hands and made life too easy for the mum, but I also think that our friends were actually thinking of Tineka in that moment, and found a quick way of moving the conversation away from her.

As we walked to our car, our friend's mother asked why Tineka was uneasy at the café with people laughing and staring at her. 'Do you feel comfortable around White people?' she asked.

'Well, I did marry a White man,' Tineka responded.

After each incident, it became harder and harder to convince Tineka to leave the house where we were staying. She was withdrawn in a way I had never seen her.

The following day, we went to the main event: the food festival. We found our team table, where we would make a local stew from scratch, and then I peeled off from the group and went with our friend to collect the meat and other ingredients. Standing there in the queue, I had a moment of panic – was Tineka OK? Were people staring at her? Did she feel safe? As a Black woman, Tineka really stood out, and I wanted to be with her so she could at least tell me if she felt uncomfortable. The last thing I wanted was to get back to the place and find her surrounded by people staring at her.

As soon as we got our ingredients, I carried the heavy bucket as fast as I could into the huge hall and found Tineka and our Romanian friend. I asked Tineka if she was OK and she told me she was uneasy. Men had come up close to her to stare and she didn't want to be alone. When I say men came up to stare at Tineka, I don't mean from afar. People would come within inches of her face and take pictures. Some of the people around us seemed to think Tineka was the entertainment, and, as I do not speak a word of Romanian, there was very little I could do about it, and we didn't want to complain too much to our local hosts, who were very proud of their hometown. So proud, in fact, that they seemed to hardly notice the attention Tineka was getting.

At 9 a.m. the competition kicked off and we got to work. We used old-school hand-powered machines to grind the meat and then cooked it with various vegetables in a pot which looked like a cauldron. We worked as a team and after a while the stew bubbled away and smelled delicious.

One of the judges, a local Romanian celebrity, was walking around the hall and meeting the teams. He came over to our table, shook Tineka's hand and asked to take pictures with her. He attracted quite a bit of attention and the encounter became a hassle.

When the other judges called him away, he whispered in my ear, 'Your wife is very beautiful.' It was hard to tell if he was being complimentary or creepy, or maybe a bit of both.

A few hours later, the judges announced the runners-up and the winners. It was in Romanian and impossible to understand. But then our friend punched the air and shouted, 'We won silver!' We were invited on stage and I was excited, but I could see Tineka was feeling something else. She was not pleased that she was going to face a crowd of people who had not won. Would the other contestants ruin the experience? I saw it differently. Whatever other people said, this was a once-in-a-lifetime moment. A weird experience, but something very unique and exciting. So I encouraged Tineka to get up on the stage, ignore everyone and just smile for the cameras.

A few days later we left Romania for the journey back home. I had seen a lot and I had a lot to process. Tineka summarised her thoughts for me: 'I am not coming back to Romania.'

Our experience in Romania was not as multicultural as other countries we have visited, and she told our friends what she thought without sugar-coating it. They insisted that the festival was not a normal situation, and that Tineka had to come back to Romania another time and visit the capital city Bucharest. Tineka thanked them for the invitation but said she did not feel comfortable and would prefer not to come.

In an attempt to convince Tineka to come back for another visit, our friend asked, 'If I invite another Black person would that make you feel better?'

I cringed. I knew they were trying to help, but they were falling into the same trap I had fallen into many times before when trying to fix things and put Tineka at ease. But despite their good intentions, they are not superheroes, and they could not solve ignorance, reverse history and instill equality in their hometown.

Although these experiences were difficult, we keep finding new places to visit and new cultures to explore. The relative calm of home life is enjoyable, but I have found it important to celebrate the road less travelled rather than get stuck in the comfortable chair. It is challenging and enriching to step away from normality and embrace new perspectives that can only be witnessed while on the road. My hope for Tineka and myself is that we continue to be strong and adventurous as a couple, and encourage each other to travel when we have a family and when we get older. That way we can continue to break down our assumptions about the world and uncover fresh perspectives on what 'normal' means.

8

BLACK WOMAN. WHITE WORLD.

TINEKA

Confession: I am not an angry Black woman. But some White colleagues turn me into one.

'The most disrespected person in America is the black woman. The most unprotected person in America is the black woman. The most neglected person in America is the black woman.'[18] This famous quote from Malcolm X is sadly still true more than a half a century later – and with police charges over the 2020 murder of George Floyd, a Black man, but no charges for the death of Breonna Taylor, a Black female EMT aspiring to be a nurse, who was shot five to six times while she slept and had no criminal record – shows the value society places on the life of a Black woman. The White police officer who shot her was only charged for bullets that landed in another apartment, a painful reminder to Black women everywhere how our worth is viewed today. But the USA isn't the only country with this attitude towards Black women and we have to survive it every day – in almost every situation and context – even in the workplace.

I find it perplexing when my colleagues become increasingly confused by my growing anger in the workplace as it becomes harder to hide. Don't they know that smart and ambitious women of colour want to climb the ladder too? But when we reach our hands to go another step, they are stomped beneath someone else's feet, ensuring we stay in place, while they use our talent and work as a source to draw strength from and continue their ascent. After numerous meetings over several months – where I have to detail my CV and name-drop projects just so my White colleagues will trust that I am intelligent enough to make decisions for the job they hired *and* headhunted me for, in addition to accolades from senior management – is it any wonder that I walk around angry? And only then do they become scared, because they have driven me to be their stereotypical 'angry Black woman'.

In some work environments I have been the person to bring cupcakes to the office. That is me, that is who I am. That annoying woman who remembers everyone's birthdays and gets excited about surprising them when they think no one knows. The one who suggests we should have a meeting outside in the sun and sneak wine out too. I am not an angry Black woman. In fact, I believe there is no such thing as an angry Black woman. We are simply reacting to the consistent and sometimes subtle, unjust treatment we receive every day. For many years in the workplace I walked around trying to take up as little space as possible. Saying 'yes' to my White colleagues, and making sure to constantly smile and appear sweet to stay in their good graces. And through experience and understanding the value of my work, and the crippling injustice of microaggressions in the workplace, I now always fight back. I do not base my decisions on pleasing White people. I am proud to be unapologetically Black and have no guilt in taking up as much space as I can when I walk into a room.

I am usually the only woman of colour in the places I work, or the only one at my experience level. This usually means that I am left to contend with the White males who try to exert their authority over me one way or another, growing ever more frustrated and aggressive as I refuse to relent. At one job I learnt to speak up more after one of my White bosses took credit for my work at an important meeting in front of me. I was speechless.

'People are like dogs,' one White male manager said to me when I told him what had happened. 'You have to flick them on the nose right away when they misbehave. If you flick them on the nose later, they won't know why you're punishing them.' While that advice might be easy for a White guy to apply in the workplace, as a Black woman, I have to be more careful. I can never mess up. Even one slip-up and I'm considered lazy and unintelligent. Or if I voice my opinion too much, I'm aggressive and difficult.

Alex has told me that I put an unnecessary amount of pressure on myself to succeed. He doesn't understand that I put it on myself not just for my own sake. I do my best to excel at work to show that all Black women can succeed and are equal to and just as smart as our White colleagues. Black women as successful leaders or excelling is still not seen as a norm by many in society. Black women are still accomplishing a lot of 'firsts'. And if we are the only ones represented in our environment, there's a sense of responsibility for paving the way for others like us. Misty Copeland, American Ballet Theatre's first Black principal dancer, and arguably the most famous ballerina today in an almost totally White industry, had this to say of her success, and being a 'first': 'I feel like I'm dancing for so many people that weren't given the opportunities that I have, so I understand my responsibility and how I'm seen and how I'm viewed. Just being on the stage is doing so much for the next generation.'

Women of colour are overlooked and challenged every day in the workplace. When a new person starts at my company, often in junior roles, they immediately challenge my decision-making authority and interestingly never question their new White colleagues. This is frustrating because at the start of every job I have to prove myself by working harder and accomplishing more than my White colleagues. So when someone new who I haven't already 'impressed' with my work asks me if I am 'really capable and have the authority to be making these decisions', it takes everything within me not to scream. And this is what I experience day in and day out – excelling at work, giving 120 per cent with very few people doing the same around me – while trying to calmly avoid junior White employees trying to tell me how to do my job, which has nothing to do with theirs, and evading senior White employees trying to claim my work as their own.

It is hard for me to be strong all the time. And there have been days I have gone home crying to Alex about the treatment I receive. In the beginning he didn't really understand, but then he would see me become physically sick by the emotional treatment I experienced and be forced to leave a workplace for the sake of my mental health, knowing that I am not a quitter.

I like to think I am a thick-skinned person, but if people are chipping away at me every day, I can only be strong for so long.

I once overheard two White male colleagues plot to have me fired, when they didn't know I was round the corner in a nearby cubicle. One of them looked up my salary when they weren't supposed to, by asking for a password from HR and lying about the reason it was needed. He had looked up *my* salary only – the only minority on the team.

'I'll just tell him we don't need her any more. She makes too much money for someone like her anyway,' one of them said.

'Yeah, but the director loves her work; she does do good work.'

'No, she needs to leave; she adds nothing to the team.' The issue wasn't my salary; the issue was my salary compared to theirs. When my director called me into his office to warn me that there 'might not' be enough budget to keep me the next year, I wasn't surprised. I was already making progress with our greetings-card business, so agreed it might be a good time to part ways. I could have fought the good fight and stayed, but I didn't want to work with people or a director who would allow that type of sentiment to fester. As I've become older, I've started to learn sometimes it's better to pick your battles and simply walk away.

Being harassed based on the colour of your skin in the workplace can be a very lonely feeling. Most of the time in the organisations I have worked for, aggressions actually stem from the human resources department. In one situation an HR assistant made stereotypical comments about Black people in my presence over the course of several months, even going so far as to tell colleagues that I was not American because of the colour of my skin, but 'just an African with an American accent'.

I finally felt obligated to speak to our directors – all of whom were White – about the comments, and we had a meeting with the HR assistant. The assistant admitted she had said racially inappropriate comments in my presence, but didn't offer any apology or explanation. Meanwhile, the White directors listened silently while shifting in their seats nervously. The directors offered no reprimand towards the HR assistant, nor did they request for an apology to be made to me. The directors were too uncomfortable with the fact of racial aggressions happening in their teams to do anything. These experiences have led me to realise that workplace institutions are not set up for people of colour to thrive; they are set up *against* people of colour, because there is often no one in a senior position willing to advocate on our behalf when we experience subtle or overt workplace discrimination. Part of that problem is also the fact that the most senior roles in the workplace are almost always held by White people.

I'm tired. I'm tired of fighting. I'm tired of having to prove myself again and again. Just to have to prove myself again and again. I'm tired of saying an idea to a room of White people in a meeting only to have them shake their heads in disagreement or give me blank stares before it has even been uttered from my lips. Only to have the White guy next to me repeat the same idea verbatim and have everyone nod and clap in agreement. For everyone White their CVs speak volumes, they can walk into a new job and have immediate respect. I am headhunted. I have glowing references from people at the top of their fields and yet I receive zero respect when I enter a new workplace.

And then when I bring visibility and recognition to the department for my work, I receive scowls. But I know if I ever made a mistake or stopped working hard, they'd scowl even more. I want them to know that Black women's lives, thoughts, ideas and careers do matter. I want to tell them that we are meant to be heard. We are not here to serve.

They don't know how alone, belittled and intimidated I feel sometimes by them. I go into work with my head and neck stretched high, and I do it for Black women in the workplace everywhere who can't. I whisper a few lines from Maya Angelou's poignant poem 'Still I Rise' to myself to get through those days:

> You may shoot me with your words,
> You may cut me with your eyes,
> You may kill me with your hatefulness
> But still, like air, I'll rise.[19]

9

BATTLING WITH THE COLOUR CONUNDRUM

TINEKA

Confession: I have learnt that racism affects us all, regardless of our skin colour.

If you really think about it – racism makes absolutely no sense. People of colour are human beings with similar thoughts, feelings, concerns and ambitions to White people. When a person is born, they don't choose their race or culture or nationality. Prejudice, bias, racism, discrimination, whatever you want to call it, is a systemic punishment of people who had no control over the identity they were born with, which the world often deems 'lesser than'. What is even more disheartening is that predominantly White societies do nothing to help fight the oppression and institutional racism that so many have to suffer from on a daily basis.

We're going through a painful awakening when it comes to race, and it's important for us to use our voices – no matter how big or how small – to continue talking about it and raise awareness about the detrimental effects it has, not just on people of colour, but on everyone.

I know that because I am in an interracial relationship, and my husband and I will never truly understand each other, not because we were born different but because of society. It has taken me some time, but I've come to realise that not fully understanding each other is OK. We can be in relationships or friendships with people we disagree with when it comes to our beliefs, as long as a level of respect and sensitivity remains. While studying anthropology at university, I learnt that all people have some type of privilege. This can be through gender, religion, sexuality, nationality and, of course, race. And those on the receiving end of said privilege often live life with blinders, which are onerous to remove.

White supremacy and racism are all-too-real villains that are embedded in our daily lives and everyday institutions. Racism breaks down the mental state of the people who are victims of it. It changes their personality entirely. You are either completely broken by it or you are forced to change into a person whose resilience is almost superhuman. Some of us have to walk through the world in a constant fight-or-flight mode. We have to constantly choose which battles to fight or run away from based on their overt or subtle severity, or the detrimental effects that standing up for ourselves will have.

When I was a child, before the realities of life hit me, I used to be a carefree person. I used to be trusting to a fault. I used to be naive about the reality of the world around me. I am not those things any longer, because of the effects and horrors that I have lived through based on the colour of my skin. Experiencing racism has taken aspects of myself away from me. In order to protect myself and my sanity I have less patience. I am less trusting. I have to stand up and fight for myself more. I am constantly thinking about whether a negative slight is based on the colour of my skin, my gender, both or neither, and to constantly have to pass through the world thinking that way is a sad thing. I don't want to do it. I don't enjoy doing it. I don't want to be strong all the time. I don't want to fight all the time. But the racism embedded in our society forces me to be this way. I want to be sweeter. I want to be kinder. I want to be more trusting. I want to be more patient. But I am not able to be those things. It is savage to refuse to see fellow people as human because of the colour of their skin. And for persons of colour to be used as a symbol of something hated is disheartening and speaks to the sadness that is our society, our reality.

Racism affects White people too. For those who wield it, it chips away at what could have been goodness within them. Racism creates a reality that is less loving, less trusting and less unified. It tricks people out of experiencing the richness of different cultures, viewpoints and personalities. It promotes a bland, cold world with no feeling or understanding of human dignity. I am proud to be a part of my Black 'race'. But I want to be even prouder to be part of the human race.

If you're White, realise you have the privilege to stand up against racism, and that your White peers will stand up and take notice. If you're a person of colour, have the courage to stand up for yourself and others who can't – knowing that you're not alone in doing so. Be open to engaging and talking to White people about race, and call them out on their behaviour when needed. We don't have to do it, and perhaps it isn't fair, but through being constantly vocal and educating those who need it, we will see start to see a change, however slow it is. We should all teach our children the beauty of difference, and that all shades of skin – no matter how dark or light – are equally beautiful and 'normal'.

I am grateful for the people of colour and White people who have made the world a better place for future generations of minorities. I reap those benefits. If we each do our small part, we honour their memory. We keep alive their hopes and dreams for a world where all races are treated as equals.

ALEX

Confession: I have learnt that I need to accept my privilege, but also my limitations.

I hope it is obvious by now that I strongly believe White people have just as much to gain in making the world a more equal place as people from other races. When everyone gets the opportunity to be heard and celebrated, we all grow as a result.

I want to encourage you to support the person you love. It is so simple, but I will say that one more time. Support the person you love. Be there for them. Celebrate them and bring your energy to your family so that they are filled with confidence and pride in who they are. This is especially important for those in a relationship with someone who is not White. No matter how hard it may be to put yourself to one side and devote your energies to someone else, this is a valuable and enriching experience. We are all responsible for improving lives around us and making the world a better place every day.

And you can support your partner even in those moments when you are confused, doubtful or uncertain. You do not need to fully understand a difficult moment to be fully part of that moment and a force for harmony in that moment. Try to take a leap of faith, embrace the unknown and feel your way through it. This is not easy. This is scary. But it is doable, and I am living proof that it is possible to fail and fail again before getting better at it. It is possible to grow your awareness, take in new learnings and become more aware of the world around you.

Please listen carefully, though. It would be a mistake to think I would encourage anyone to neglect themselves and their beliefs. I am not saying White people in general or White people in interracial relationships specifically need to suppress themselves and go through the world agreeing with the person they are with. I am saying learn about yourself – don't lose yourself. Do not run away from these big topics and do not pretend these challenging moments will disappear. Find that sweet spot where you are working together, finding commonality and bringing strength and confidence to each other.

Coming to terms with my own inadequacies and my lack of understanding has been tough, as you have seen.

I have had to accept that I have misjudged situations and misunderstood interactions, and that was not easy to do, because my pride got in the way; my perspective was too rigid. I had to take Tineka's frustrations and work with them before I could move on and see things in a particular way.

I had to recognise that White privilege is real. I had to get over this huge White privilege hump before I could accept that my upbringing and my racial context has blinded me from seeing certain situations as racially charged in the same way Tineka does. You might be so used to wearing that privilege every day that you cannot feel it or see it. So when your partner hears a comment and identifies it as racially motivated, I encourage you to hold that possibility as a real option. To your ears the comment might sound snarky or insensitive, but maybe it was more than that. Maybe. And it is OK to not know immediately; it is OK to ask questions, challenge your understanding and be open to learning what you did not hear.

That doesn't mean I think you need to pay for the sins of previous generations. You can't influence the past, but you can play a part in influencing the future, even if that future is only lived by one person. And to do that all I am saying is you need to realise that your experience is influenced by the past, which you had no control over. Accepting that allowed me to see that I had some severe limitations in my perspective. I thought for a while that meant I was somehow at a disadvantage, somehow mentally weaker, less 'woke'. What I came to learn, in fact, is that the opposite is true. By listening to a radically different perspective from my own I was able to wake myself up and target my energies towards strengthening myself in my particularly weak spots. This doesn't mean I have eliminated all weak spots. As some areas of my racial consciousness become stronger, I realise there are other areas where I need to dedicate time – the specific lessons I need to learn in order to improve the way I am a supportive spouse, a better friend and a more aware person.

Through this process allow yourself to grow internally. And I want you to know I found this to be a slow process. Painfully slow. I didn't change overnight. I didn't marry Tineka and then wake up with all the tools I need to be with her in a true sense. Gaining these tools and adapting my understanding took time, but it also took really difficult conversations, and that is OK. Conflict is real, and conflict can be a powerful way of discovering who you are and who the person you love is. Conflict can be tough, but conflict can also be respectful. Conflict and violence are very different things. Tineka may well be my soulmate, someone who I am supposed to travel through life with, but we see things very differently; we do not naturally agree all the time, and that can be tough.

I want to tell you I miss the simplicity of how life used to be for me. I would never have inspected and analysed situations in the way I do now, casual, friendly situations, even when I am chilling out on the sofa and watching a film, I have a second lens on standby mode: a latent racial awareness. I still fail to recognise moments where privilege and inequality are presented in a subtle disguise. But I have a reactionary sense that is alive in me, which was not there before. It is annoying, but I am glad it is forming within me.

To those people reading this who are not White, I also have a reminder for you – your patience matters. If you can be just a little understanding, a little forgiving, you can be a powerful force for educating others like me. We should know, we ought to know, but sometimes we fall down. I don't ask you to tolerate ignorance or to bite your tongue. I ask you to help your White friends, colleagues and family members see that they too can play a meaningful role in breaking down inequality.

Let's keep growing, let's learn about one another, and let's not pretend things are perfect. We are all prone to acting in an insensitive way, but bring an awareness to that. When that possibility is your focus, you can be a refreshing and rejuvenating force, benefiting yourself, your spouse and those around you.

ACKNOWLEDGEMENTS

We would like to jointly thank and recognise all of the hard work that has gone into *Mixed Up*.

Thank you to our agency Georgina Capel Associates and to our agent Irene Baldoni. Irene, you are a powerhouse. We know we couldn't have gone this far without you. Thank you for always listening with a critical ear and not holding back what you really think. You are more than a literary agent – you're our fairy book mother! And we would never have met our agent without the introduction from our friends Gianluca and Viola – thank you both.

To Katie Packer, our badass editor, thank you for all of your work on pushing to bring our story to a new audience and embracing the way we chose to tell it as well as your deep belief that ours is a story everyone needs to hear. And to the *Mixed Up* team at Headline publishing – Ellie and Jess thank you for your amazing marketing and PR work during a global pandemic! Your support and energy really made us feel embraced by the entire Headline family.

Thank you to Harriet Poland, Victoria Haslam, Victoria Pepe, AK Connor and Alice Morgan who championed

Mixed Up as an Audible Original and helped us find our voices.

And a final thank you to everyone who has worked behind the scenes – there are too many people to name. We are super grateful to you all.

TINEKA

In no particular order, I would like to thank the following people:

Mom and Dad, you are a constant support in everything that I do and thank you for giving me the opportunities to be able to thrive in a world that often pushes back if you don't have the right skin colour. Thank you for raising me to have a voice and for accepting that it's OK even if you don't agree with what I have to say. Mom, a special thank you for fostering a love of books and writing in me from a young age. This book wouldn't have been possible without the constant advice, enthusiasm and comfort you provided to Alex and me when others tried to stop us from telling our truth.

To all my family in the States, I love you and miss you! Thank you for all the messages of being proud and the encouragement to keep pushing for change and awareness with the book no matter how unpopular. I'm so appreciative to all of you for welcoming Alex into the family with open arms and treating him as one of your own still. And a special thank you to my late Uncle Jimmy who was the person that encouraged me to step out of my own limitations and to live abroad.

Thank you to all of my friends aka second family in the US, London and Geneva (you know who you are!) but especially Akshata, Nicole and the 'Lovely Ladies' for the constant support over the development of this book and encouragement when any negativity came my way, I am forever grateful for our friendship.

A special thank you to the mentors who fuelled my love of literature and language, Dr Kwaku Gyasi and Dr Monroe.

Last but not least a special shout-out to the interracial couples who reached out to us and shared their stories after hearing the Audible Original. Thank you for letting us know we aren't alone in our journey. I see you.

ALEX

I'd like to say a big thank you to my family for all the love you have shown me and all the support you have given us as a couple. A special shout-out to my little sister Eli who makes me so proud and never fails to remind me just how human I am.

To Jen and Max, and my cousins Celia, Lisa and their families, thank you for all of the messages and for truly supporting Tineka and me as we have gone through all the stages of bringing *Mixed Up* into the world. You have encouraged us both so much.

To my incredible in-laws and especially to Vanessa, Mike, Diane and Darrylena – thank you for accepting me into your family. You guys are so full of life and realness. I have so much to learn from y'all.

The late Jillian Hocking who was an incredible person, an inspiration who made me see it is possible to carve out a career which I love.

Thank you to my friends who I am lucky to know. These are people who have been there through so many parts of life and stuck with me as I've tried to figure things out: Patrick 'mon pote' Combley, Jonny and Krzys – who are 'harshest on those they love' and Oscar 'Butros' Lopez. Devika 'Masi' Tandon Nair and Muhammad Darwish – you guys are just the best.

Mentors who have encouraged me, read words I have put together and coached me on how to tell stories: Jonathan Clayton, Don Murray, Christopher Reardon, Hassan Arouni, Stephanie Busari and John Mazur. Thank you for sharing your wisdom and your experience.

RECOMMENDED READING LIST

Nonfiction and fiction books on racism, interracial relationships and racial identity.

The Color of Water by James McBride

The Bluest Eye by Toni Morrison

The Girl Who Fell from the Sky by Heidi Durrow

Raceless by Georgina Lawton

Caucasia by Danzy Senna

Biracial Britain by Remi Adekoya

Born A Crime by Trevor Noah

The Vanishing Half by Brit Bennett

The Hate U Give by Angie Thomas

Americanah by Chimamanda Ngozi Adichie

What White People Can Do Next by Emma Dabiri

MIXED UP

Why I'm No Longer Talking to White People About Race by Reni Eddo-Lodge

I'm Still Here by Austin Channing Brown

The Henna Wars by Abida Jaigirdar

Days of Distraction by Alexandra Chang

ENDNOTES

Introduction

1 Rachel Johnson, 'Sorry Harry, but your beautiful bolter has failed my Mum Test', *Mail Online* (6 Nov. 2016), https://www.dailymail.co.uk/debate/article-3909362/RACHEL-JOHNSON-Sorry-Harry-beautiful-bolter-failed-Mum-Test.html.

2 Melanie McDonagh, 'Prince Harry and Meghan Markle: the union of royalty and showbiz', *The Spectator* (27 Nov. 2017), https://www.spectator.co.uk/article/prince-harry-and-meghan-markle-the-union-of-royalty-and-showbiz.

Chapter 1

3 Brigitte Vittrup, 'How silence can breed prejudice: A child development professor explains how and why to talk to kids about race', *The Washington Post* (6 July 2015), https://www.washingtonpost.com/news/parenting/wp/2015/07/06/how-silence-can-breed-prejudice-a-child-development-professor-explains-how-and-why-to-talk-to-kids-about-race/.

Chapter 2

4 Dr Peggy McIntosh, 'White Privilege: Unpacking the Invisible Knapsack', *Peace and Freedom Magazine* (July 1989), https://nationalseedproject.org/Key-SEED-Texts/white-privilege-unpacking-the-invisible-knapsack.

5 Wendell Pierce, *Desert Island Discs*, BBC (27 Oct. 2019), https://www.bbc.co.uk/sounds/play/m0009ryj.

6 Charles M. Blow, 'Denying Racism Supports It', *The New York Times* (21 July 2019), https://www.nytimes.com/2019/07/21/opinion/trump-racism.html?searchResultPosition=1.

Chapter 3

7 Lupita Nyong'o (2019), *BBC Newsnight*, https://www.bbc.co.uk/news/entertainment-arts-49976837.

Chapter 4

8 Dr Peggy McIntosh, 'White Privilege and Male Privilege: A Personal Account of Coming to see Correspondences through Work in Women's Studies' *Working Paper 189* (1988), Wellesley Centers for Women, https://www.wcwonline.org/images/pdf/White_Privilege_and_Male_Privilege_Personal_Account-Peggy_McIntosh.pdf.

Chapter 5

9 Charles Pulliam-Moore, 'How "woke" went from black activist watchword to teen internet slang', Splinter (1 Aug. 2016), https://splinternews.com/how-woke-went-from-black-activist-watchword-to-teen-int-1793853989.

10 Barack Obama (2019), 'Barack Obama takes on "woke" call-out culture: "That's not activism"', *The Guardian*, https://www.youtube.com/watch?v=qaHLd8de6nM&feature=youtu.be.

11 Katherine Fugate, 'White People Are Broken', *Medium* (22 Aug. 2018), https://blog.usejournal.com/white-people-are-broken-ab0fe873e5d3.

Chapter 6

12 Ashley Graham (2018), *Pretty Big Deal*, https://stylecaster.com/ashley-graham-black-interracial-children-privilege/.

13 Ta-Nehisi Coates, *Between the World and Me*, (Text Publishing Company, 2015).

14 Kassidy Mi'chal, 'The Parents of Mixed-Race Children Must Understand THIS Vital Fact', Eye for Ebony (12 Dec. 2017), https://medium.com/@KassidyCreates/the-responsibility-of-parents-of-mixed-race-children-ff7c6dc7b115.

15 Lukwesa Burak, Twitter (20 May 2019), https://twitter.com/LukwesaBurak/status/1130523698799235072.

Chapter 7

16 Pico Iyer, 'Why We Travel', Adventure Travel News (9 Oct. 2013), https://www.adventuretravelnews.com/why-we-travel-by-pico-iyer.

17 Jeneé Osterheldt, 'Black, American, and abroad? Racism travels free', The *Boston Globe* (4 Sept. 2019), https://www.bostonglobe.com/lifestyle/travel/2019/09/04/black-american-and-abroad-racism-travels-free/UGdYCnPr7rt1R4BlVVEk3I/story.html.

18 Malcolm X (1962), https://www.washingtonpost.com/opinions/black-women-deserve-better-will-2019-be-the-year-of-change/2019/01/09/fc40e842-1439-11e9-803c-4ef28312c8b9_story.html.

Chapter 8

19 Maya Angelou, *The Complete Collected Poems of Maya Angelou*, (Virago, 1985).